I0015260

Cloud Solution Architect's Career Master Plan

Proven techniques and effective tips to help you become
a successful solution architect

Rick Weyenberg

Kyle Burns

Cloud Solution Architect's Career Master Plan

Copyright © 2024 Packt Publishing

All rights reserved. No part of this book may be reproduced, stored in a retrieval system, or transmitted in any form or by any means, without the prior written permission of the publisher, except in the case of brief quotations embedded in critical articles or reviews.

Every effort has been made in the preparation of this book to ensure the accuracy of the information presented. However, the information contained in this book is sold without warranty, either express or implied. Neither the authors, nor Packt Publishing or its dealers and distributors, will be held liable for any damages caused or alleged to have been caused directly or indirectly by this book.

Packt Publishing has endeavored to provide trademark information about all of the companies and products mentioned in this book by the appropriate use of capitals. However, Packt Publishing cannot guarantee the accuracy of this information.

Group Product Manager: Preet Ahuja

Publishing Product Manager: Nitin Nainani

Book Project Manager: Sonam Pandey

Senior Editor: Nathanya Dias

Technical Editor: Reenish Kulshrestha

Copy Editor: Safis Editing

Proofreader: Safis Editing

Indexer: Hemangini Bari

Production Designer: Joshua Misquitta

Senior Developer Relations Marketing Executive: Linda Pearlson

DevRel Marketing Coordinator: Rohan Dobhal

First published: March 2024

Production reference: 1220224

Published by Packt Publishing Ltd.

Grosvenor House

11 St Paul's Square

Birmingham

B3 1RB, UK.

ISBN 978-1-80512-971-4

www.packtpub.com

Contributors

About the authors

Rick Weyenberg, with over 25 years of professional development, design, and architecture experience, is an Azure principal cloud solution architect at Microsoft, where he leverages his expertise in cloud-based solution design and development to help companies harness the full power of the Azure cloud platform.

His current mission is to help create smarter, safer cars and reliable autonomous vehicles by leading technical architecture discussions with senior customer executives, enterprise architects, IT management, and engineers, and working with a wide variety of Azure services and platforms, ranging from **Infrastructure-as-a-Service (IaaS)** to serverless and **Platform-as-a-Service (PaaS)** offerings.

To my awesome family, thanks for the encouragement and support throughout the process. Also, thanks for always letting me nerd out.

Kyle Burns is an application developer, architect, and technical leader with over 25 years of experience delivering business and technical capabilities to enhance customer and user experience and building and directing impactful software engineering teams. He effectively utilizes platforms and established methodologies to ensure that engineered solutions meet the requirements for security, scale, reuse, and high availability and collaborates across business units, with peers and leadership, to ensure objectives, goals, and standards are aligned. Kyle is recognized as an agile thought leader who articulates and communicates technical vision and translates that vision into business acumen and is currently a principal cloud solution architect in the Microsoft Customer Success organization.

I would like to thank my amazing wife, Lisa, for her support in all of the experiences leading to the writing of this book.

About the reviewers

Thiago Born is a seasoned cloud computing professional with a rich 20+ year career, bringing expertise in cloud architecture, big data, stream analytics, and cloud-based solutions. Having worked with industry giants such as AWS and Microsoft, Thiago has delivered transformative cloud solutions to financial institutions, research organizations, and leading retail brands. His passion lies in helping businesses leverage the power of cloud computing to optimize operations, enhance scalability, and gain a competitive edge.

Matt Lunzer is married to his beautiful wife, Sara, and together they have three wonderful children, Amelia, Joseph, and Sophia. In his professional life, Matt is a seasoned cloud architect focused on the areas of hybrid and **cloud-native infrastructure and cyber security (CISSP)** while actively learning about artificial intelligence. Matt is currently employed as a technology specialist at Microsoft Corporation, assisting software companies and independent software vendors with growing and transforming their products and services on the Azure cloud platform. Matt has also contributed to a cloud-focused YouTube series, contributed to Azure architecture documentation, written blogs, and published code artifacts on GitHub.

Table of Contents

Part 2: Pursuing the Role

3

4

5

Part 3: Prepare for and After the Offer

6

Time to Pursue the Job   85

7

Interviewing – Trust the Process   99

8

Don't Forget to Give Back   113

Preface

Welcome to *Cloud Solution Architect's Career Master Plan*! This book is the go-to resource for any individual looking to start or continue a career as a solution architect designing workloads targeting cloud computing platforms. The content is based on years of experience designing cloud solutions on different platforms and under various requirements. While not all cloud platform providers are specifically mentioned, the career paths laid forth are applicable to the other providers not mentioned.

Who this book is for

If you are a self-motivated IT professional and would like to pursue a career as a solution architect, then this book is for you. You should have a solid base of traditional software architecture understanding, but not in-depth cloud concepts and design considerations.

This book will also be valuable for anyone who is considering a solution architect role as a potential career field but doesn't know where to get started. No experience in the cloud architect role is needed to get started.

What this book covers

Chapter 1, *Understanding the Responsibilities of a Cloud Solution Architect*, explains the genesis of the role of the **Cloud Solution Architect** (**CSA**), core concepts every CSA should understand, and the pros and cons of being a CSA. Specific technology domains to master are also explored, as well as common software products used to design workloads targeting a cloud provider platform.

Chapter 2, *Types of Cloud Solution Architect Roles*, explores the primary technology domains to master of the many potential areas of specialization for a CSA. Also explored are common concepts relevant to all CSAs when creating solutions for the cloud.

Chapter 3, *Education Paths to the Cloud Solution Architect Role*, addresses the fact that, for the aspiring CSA, education can come in many different forms – both formal and informal. This chapter provides various educational options to gain knowledge of cloud computing and various design considerations.

Chapter 4, *Getting Real Experience*, discusses the importance of getting experience to build upon your education and looks at various ways that a new or aspiring cloud solution architect can build experience.

Chapter 5, *Closing In on Opportunities*, provides guidance around focusing on specific industries, deciding the optimal size and maturity of a company and whether traditional IT is a good fit, and resources to find opportunities worth pursuing.

Chapter 6, *Time to Pursue the Job*, looks at knowing what experience level to pursue, reasonable compensation goals, how to optimize your online presence, and preparing for the process – all steps in preparation for the interview process. Each of these topics is covered in this chapter.

Chapter 7, *Interviewing – Trust the Process*, explores strategies for successfully navigating the CSA job interview, including common questions and scenarios – provided in this chapter as a way to prepare for a successful outcome.

Chapter 8, *Don't Forget to Give Back*, talks about having a lasting impact on the tech community and society in general.

To get the most out of this book

This book focuses on the general requirements and demands of a cloud solution architect. As such, the tools needed to complement the content are a computing device and access to the internet via a browser to follow recommended websites for more information.

Download the example code files

We also have other code bundles from our rich catalog of books and videos available at `https://github.com/PacktPublishing/`. Check them out!

Conventions used

There are a number of text conventions used throughout this book.

`Code in text`: Indicates code words in text, database table names, folder names, filenames, file extensions, pathnames, dummy URLs, user input, and Twitter handles. Here is an example: "By convention, open source projects hosted on GitHub tend to have the following documents in the root of the repository that consumers and contributors to the project should be familiar with:

- `CODE_OF_CONDUCT.md`
- `CONTRIBUTING.md...`"

Bold: Indicates a new term, an important word, or words that you see onscreen. For instance, words in menus or dialog boxes appear in **bold**. Here is an example: "Navigate via the browser to `https://aws.amazon.com/` and click on the text that reads **Create an AWS Account** in the upper-right corner of the page."

> **Tips or important notes**
> Appear like this.

Get in touch

Feedback from our readers is always welcome.

General feedback: If you have questions about any aspect of this book, email us at customercare@ packtpub.com and mention the book title in the subject of your message.

Errata: Although we have taken every care to ensure the accuracy of our content, mistakes do happen. If you have found a mistake in this book, we would be grateful if you would report this to us. Please visit www.packtpub.com/support/errata and fill in the form.

Piracy: If you come across any illegal copies of our works in any form on the internet, we would be grateful if you would provide us with the location address or website name. Please contact us at copyright@packt.com with a link to the material.

If you are interested in becoming an author: If there is a topic that you have expertise in and you are interested in either writing or contributing to a book, please visit authors.packtpub.com.

Share your thoughts

Once you've read *Cloud Solution Architect's Career Master Plan*, we'd love to hear your thoughts! Scan the QR code below to go straight to the Amazon review page for this book and share your feedback.

https://packt.link/r/1-805-12971-6

Your review is important to us and the tech community and will help us make sure we're delivering excellent quality content

Download a free PDF copy of this book

Thanks for purchasing this book!

Do you like to read on the go but are unable to carry your print books everywhere?

Is your eBook purchase not compatible with the device of your choice?

Don't worry, now with every Packt book you get a DRM-free PDF version of that book at no cost.

Read anywhere, any place, on any device. Search, copy, and paste code from your favorite technical books directly into your application.

The perks don't stop there, you can get exclusive access to discounts, newsletters, and great free content in your inbox daily

Follow these simple steps to get the benefits:

1. Scan the QR code or visit the link below

https://packt.link/free-ebook/9781805129714

2. Submit your proof of purchase

3. That's it! We'll send your free PDF and other benefits to your email directly

Part 1:
Introduction to the Cloud Solution Architect Role

This part of the book will be an introduction to the role of cloud solution architect. We'll look at where we are today, how we got here, and what it really means to be a cloud solution architect. Also, we'll discuss the options we have when pursuing a cloud solution architect role and tradeoffs to consider between those options.

This part has the following chapters:

1

Understanding the Responsibilities of a Cloud Solution Architect

Cloud computing has its roots in foundational capabilities, available as early as the 1950s. Because of these enabling technologies as well as more recent advancements, the need for an architect to design workload solutions optimized for the cloud is a highly demanded skill set today. This architect's role started as a **solution architect (SA)**, but as time evolved and cloud computing continued to mature, a new type of architect was needed to address the new paradigm of cloud computing. The last 10-15 years have created an opportunity for architects to specialize in cloud-native (cloud only) and hybrid cloud architecture. This role became known as a **cloud SA (CSA)**.

To understand the current role of a CSA and what it takes to become one, we need to do some level-setting. In this chapter, we will learn what a CSA does by first providing a brief history of cloud computing and its relationship to the increasing demand for CSAs. Next, we will examine the foundational requirements for a successful CSA. The third section will address the reality of the CSA role and some of the trade-offs when working with an ever-changing, evolving ecosystem. At this point, we will discuss potential areas of specialty that a CSA can explore and what responsibilities to expect. Finally, we will explore the tools that CSAs use in their daily lives to design, deploy, and support workloads in the cloud. By the end of this chapter, you will have a deep understanding of the role of CSA and will be able to decide on an area of expertise that fits with your desired career path.

In this chapter, we will cover the following topics:

- The evolution of cloud computing
- Common cloud concepts
- Introducing the CSA
- Upsides and downsides of being a CSA
- Role-specific cloud technology domains to consider as a career path
- Recommended productivity tools for CSAs

Technical requirements

Later in this chapter, productivity tools are discussed as a part of the role of CSA. To get access to the various tools and platforms mentioned, here is a list of locations where cloud provider platforms and tools can be accessed:

- *Amazon Web Services (AWS) account*: Navigate via the browser to `https://aws.amazon.com/` and click on the image that reads **Create an AWS Account** in the upper-right corner of the page
- *Microsoft Azure subscription*: Navigate via the browser to `https://azure.microsoft.com/` and click on the image that reads **Free account** in the upper-right corner of the page
- *Google Cloud Platform (GCP) account*: Navigate via the browser to `https://cloud.google.com/` and click on the image that reads **Start free** in the upper-right corner of the page
- *Lucidchart*: Navigate via the browser to `https://www.lucidchart.com/` and click on the image that reads **Sign up free** in the upper-right corner of the page
- *Visio*: Navigate via the browser to `https://www.microsoft.com/en-us/microsoft-365/visio/flowchart-software/` and click on the image that reads **See plans and pricing** on the left side of the page
- *Microsoft Visual Studio Code (VS Code)*: Navigate via the browser to `https://code.visualstudio.com/download` and click on the image with text that represents your operating system (Windows, Linux, or Mac) in the middle of the page

The evolution of cloud computing

To appreciate and understand the role of CSA better, we should begin with a timeline of cloud computing to see how/why the industry needed this role. Cloud computing democratically offers computing capabilities and services via the internet. It has evolved generationally from the ideation of several foundational concepts and principles over roughly the last 60-70 years to current and emerging technologies. **Artificial intelligence (AI)** and **quantum computing (QC)** are currently at the center of shaping the ongoing evolution of cloud computing:

1950s – History tends to repeat itself, and cloud computing is no exception. One of the cloud's attractive characteristics is the fact that the consumer of cloud services only pays for what they use. This harkens back to the 1950s when gigantic mainframes were shared by leasing time through the terminals connected to them. Fast-forward to the present, and this aligns with the responsibility of the CSA role, which is cost optimization by provisioning and deprovisioning cloud services as demand dictates.

- **1960s** – A networking technology was created by the U.S. Department of Defense called **Advanced Research Projects Agency Network (ARPANET)** that later went on to become the basis for the modern internet. Understanding private and public network constructs is critical for a CSA as this is the foundational layer of separation for a cloud computing workload.

- **1970s** – Another critical capability leveraged by cloud computing came along in the 1970s, called **virtual machines (VMs)**. IBM created a technology that allowed multiple virtual operating systems to be run on the same physical system. This eventually enabled the hypervisor software, which made a cluster of physical nodes look like a single physical node that hosted these connected VMs. On cloud computing platforms, compute cycles, storage, and other services are exposed by cloud providers at the hypervisor level. A CSA needs to be aware of restrictions placed on the guest operating systems they provision.

- **1980s** – This was a quiet time, except for personal computers beginning to show up in people's homes. As technology advanced, form factors shrank, and costs went down. At the time, they were used mostly for word processing and playing games. For a CSA, a PC/laptop enables the use of various tools to design, code, and test solutions, many of which we will describe in a later section.

- **1990s** – The internet (a successor to ARPANET mentioned previously) became widely available and popular from the late 1990s to the early 2000s. Companies such as Amazon, Google, and Salesforce started to offer web-based services and applications that customers could access without installing any software on their devices. The internet is the last introduction and adoption of technology needed to enable cloud computing. CSAs understand that the internet enables access to their workload privately or publicly, as well as other people or systems. Because of this enablement, understanding security needs is a critical skill for a CSA.

Figure 1.1 shows a sample cloud architecture from the late 2000s on Microsoft's Azure cloud platform:

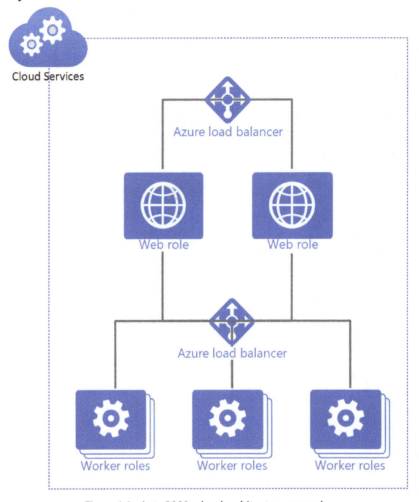

Figure 1.1 – Late 2000s cloud architecture example

- **2000s** – By the mid-2000s, cloud computing began to surface as a platform. In 2006, Amazon launched its **Elastic Compute Cloud (EC2)** and **Simple Storage Service (S3)** services, which let users rent virtual servers and storage space on demand. Google followed suit with its App Engine service in 2008, which enabled developers to build and host web applications on Google's infrastructure. Microsoft also joined the cloud market with its Azure platform in 2013. Since then, cloud computing has grown rapidly and diversified into various deployment models that serve diverse needs and preferences of users. *Figure 1.2* shows a sample cloud architecture from the present on Amazon's AWS cloud platform:

Figure 1.2 – 2023 cloud architecture example

CSAs now exist because of this era of computing technology. Cloud providers provide network, compute, storage, and other services used by CSAs to enable hyperscale workloads that are resilient, secure, and performant.

The current era is unfolding in front of us, bringing innovation and disruptive technologies for the future while enhancing existing services and products. Some of these include containers, serverless computing, edge computing, multi-cloud environments, AI, blockchain, QC, and so on. These technologies improve the performance, scalability, security, efficiency, and functionality of cloud services for various use cases and domains.

This continual evolution of cloud computing is the reason CSAs continue to learn, adapt, and apply new concepts and understanding of cloud computing capabilities. CSAs are trained to be learn-it-all instead of know-it-all. Being a know-it-all is almost impossible, with today's cloud providers offering hundreds of services each.

Even though there are potentially hundreds of services available to a CSA via a specific cloud provider, there are some concepts that are universal. Now, we will explore those concepts.

Common cloud concepts

In this section, we need to cover common cloud concepts and some misconceptions that still exist today. There is a base level of understanding regarding cloud computing and cloud providers that a CSA needs to provide workloads that are optimized for cost, availability, supportability, performance, and security. The following topics will be discussed to achieve a base level of understanding for a CSA.

Today, there are many cloud computing providers globally. As identified previously, AWS (https://aws.amazon.com), Microsoft Azure (https://www.azure.com), and GCP (https://cloud.google.com) are the three top providers by market share. There are other providers in the cloud computing space, such as IBM, Oracle, Salesforce, and Alibaba, but this book will focus on the top three since the skills are completely transferrable from one cloud provider to another unless otherwise mentioned.

Cloud service models

Within cloud computing, three common cloud service models exist to enable different levels of abstraction to the underlying infrastructure. This allows customers to satisfy potential requirements to have control of each layer of the provided infrastructure. There are three main types of service models, which are explained next:

- **Infrastructure as a Service (IaaS)** is the first service type and has existed the longest out of all the models. With IaaS, the cloud user has access to the guest operating system and anything installed with that VM. Cloud users do not have access to the hypervisor and below in most cases.

- **Platform as a Service (PaaS)** is the next level of abstraction from the cloud provider's platform. With PaaS, the cloud user is no longer accessing the guest operating system. This creates less operational overhead for the cloud user than with IaaS, but it also restricts the configuration and control of the guest operating system.

- **Software as a Service (SaaS)** is the top level of abstraction. In this model, software and all the supporting infrastructure are delivered to the cloud user, usually over the internet. With the SaaS model, the cloud user can customize the solution only at the application level, in most cases by configuration. It is also common for a SaaS provider to deliver integration APIs for the ingress and egress of information within the application.

To understand the differences between the aforementioned models, *Figure 1.3* depicts which components of the cloud provider infrastructures the cloud user is responsible for and what the cloud provider manages. This is known as the **shared responsibility model (SRM)**:

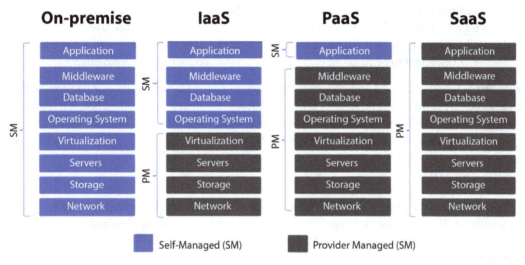

Figure 1.3 – SRM

As mentioned previously, responsibility or control needed over an infrastructure layer in the three aforementioned models will determine which model a customer selects. In addition to software or operating system requirements determining the selected service model, the overall solution architecture *deployment* model may drive the decision as well. Some cloud customers elect to keep some products or services running on-premises, while others may spread a solution across multiple cloud platforms. The physical location of services or products and the nature of interaction will likely drive the service model selected. Let's now explore the various deployment models.

Cloud deployment models

A cloud deployment model is recognized by where components of the solution architecture are deployed. The first model is the **cloud-native** model and is likely the most flexible for service model selection. This model is represented when all components of a solution architecture are provisioned within a cloud platform. In most situations, a cloud-native deployment model does not require a specific service model to be adopted. IaaS, PaaS, and SaaS can all be viable candidates.

Next, a more complex model is called the **hybrid cloud** model. This model is represented by deploying some components running on-premises and some running on a cloud provider's platform. For the components to interact with each other, a secure connection between locations is recommended. This level of connection typically requires an IaaS or a PaaS service model, given the need to control logical network access and security between locations.

The multi-cloud model is almost identical to the hybrid cloud one, except components will run on multiple cloud platforms instead of on-premises. Given the similar requirements for secure connectivity as a hybrid cloud model, IaaS and PaaS service models are leading candidates.

Hybrid cloud and multi-cloud deployment models add the most complexity to the task of designing solutions for a CSA due to the responsibility and ownership of the infrastructure layers. A CSA will need to understand all infrastructure locations, what type of connectivity exists between them, and what security rules need to be enforced to create a successful contract within deployments.

Regardless of the service model or deployment model selected, cloud security is another universal topic across all cloud providers. While security is not specifically shown as a layer in the SRM, it should be assumed that any layer the CSA has access to requires secure configuration, access, and management. Let's explore cloud security concepts in the next section.

Cloud security

Because security in the cloud is so important, most cloud providers have security baselines for each service offered. These baselines are based on industry and regulatory best practices and should not be ignored. When considering security requirements, the following should be a requirement for every solution a CSA designs:

- **Just-in-Time (JIT) access** – Only allow access to cloud resources when they are needed. Standing access should not be allowed.

- **Least-privilege access** – Provide just enough authority so that a job can be done. Do not provide the keys to the castle.

- **Assumed breach** – Always assume the system has been compromised. Then, figure out how to limit the blast radius.

- **Zero Trust** – Assume a user is being impersonated and do not trust them. This requires enforcement of authentication, authorization, and entitlements.

In addition to the aforementioned considerations, periodic security scans of the cloud should be performed to ensure that the solution is security-compliant. Some cloud providers come with services to help with scans, and they should be used wherever possible.

While cloud security is extremely important, a close second is cost control. CSAs need to ensure that any solution architectures follow a reasonable cost model. Let's discuss cloud costs next.

Cloud costs

On the surface, cost may seem a less important consideration than other decisions such as what service to use, what security controls to implement, and so on. However, if cost is not considered as part of the solution architecture, then the budget for the workload could be blown, or ongoing support costs could become extremely high. Cloud providers have various cost models they offer to the customer. The most common are pay-as-you-go (pay as you consume the cloud service) and reserved instances (prepay for cloud services you are confident you will consume over time). Costs can also be negotiated between the cloud customer and the cloud provider.

The important thing to understand is regardless of the cost models, cost controls need to be built into the solution architecture by the CSA. Most cloud providers provide pricing calculators, cost estimators, and budgeting services to help provide visibility on costs and budgets. Also, most cloud providers provide frameworks, with specific guidance related to costs and cost optimization, as well as many other topics.

Cloud frameworks

The **Cloud Adoption Framework** (**CAF**) is a collection of white papers, reference architectures, costing/budgeting tools, and other resources to help create a strategy for adopting cloud computing across an enterprise. The framework is quite comprehensive and covers everything from data classification to application portfolio assessment guidance, and many other topics that will influence an enterprise in making data-driven decisions. The CAF is essential for a CSA working with enterprises and organizations that are new to cloud computing, as well as existing cloud consumers to stay positioned to continue to implement new features and services at scale.

An example of an enterprise workload deployed on Microsoft's Azure platform following CAF best practices can be seen in *Figure 1.4*:

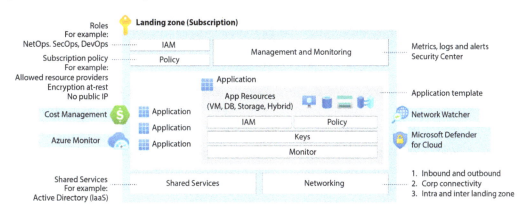

Figure 1.4 – CAF sample

Each cloud platform takes a unique approach to presenting the CAF as each provider has different perspectives.

The **Well-Architected Framework (WAF)** is a continuation of the CAF. Within the solution architecture design and development processes, the WAF ensures that the solution is well architected and aligns with best practices within the cloud computing domain and the cloud provider domain. Every solution provisioned to a cloud platform should include a WAF assessment. This will help expose any areas that require additional work to make the solution cloud-ready, according to industry standards and best practices. Typically, each cloud provider will provide a set of recommendations for a WAF, with specific consideration for their specific platform. One example of a comprehensive WAF approach, including considerations and available assessment tools, can be found on Microsoft Azure's documentation site here: `https://learn.microsoft.com/en-us/azure/architecture/framework/`.

The continued evolution of cloud computing, combined with common cloud concepts, plays a significant part in the responsibilities associated with the role of CSA. In this next section, let's finally introduce the role of CSA and see how this continues to shape day-to-day responsibilities.

Introducing the CSA

The evolution of cloud computing has created a demand for a new type of SA: a CSA. Cloud consumers eventually realized that cloud computing is more nuanced than on-premises. Architects made certain assumptions about the infrastructure when architecting on-premises solutions. For example, concepts such as network faults rarely got considered in solution design due to the infrequency of the faults happening. If a network outage, intermittent or not, made a database inaccessible, the client trying to connect to the database would try once and then fail. Transient network faults happen from time to time in the cloud, and architects need to design around these faults. The cloud has many other examples of different considerations, all of which have helped define the role of CSA.

A traditional SA focuses on on-premises solutions, while a CSA extends their role to the cloud. A CSA designs and develops platforms and applications for various organizations that use cloud-based technologies. They also collaborate with other teams, such as infrastructure, cloud, security engineering, and compliance, to provide cloud security baselines and industry best practices. A variety of capabilities and skills are required of the CSA to do their job effectively. Let us explore those capabilities in this section.

A primary responsibility of a CSA is to express their solutions to various persons within the organization. From engineers to business stakeholders, each person associated with a cloud solution or workload will have some sort of collaboration with the CSA. To make these interactions as productive as possible, verbal and written skills will allow them to share and consume information in an effective manner.

A CSA needs to write code and/or scripts in any language that the selected cloud platform supports. This follows the **Infrastructure-as-Code (IaC)** model, whereby resources are created and destroyed in the cloud by running code and/or scripts. This paradigm allows a CSA to express cloud workloads as code that gets executed to provision and configure all customer services and infrastructure to support their workload. This fits well with the **continuous integration/continuous deployment (CI/CD)** strategy and DevSecOps and enables the customer to create immutable infrastructure so that they can de-provision and re-provision simply by rerunning the code. This can be cost-saving if the resources are not required to be always up in scenarios such as testing environments.

CSAs need to understand cloud networking and infrastructure to effectively design and manage cloud computing systems for an organization. These are the components and services that enable cloud-based applications and data storage. Frontend platforms, backend platforms, cloud-based delivery systems, and cloud networks are part of cloud networking and infrastructure. Understanding these elements helps CSAs ensure that the cloud architecture is scalable, secure, reliable, and cost-efficient.

To protect cloud computing systems and data from unauthorized access, breaches, and attacks, a CSA needs to follow cybersecurity guidance and best practices. A CSA can use cybersecurity guidance and best practices to identify security and compliance requirements, select appropriate cloud models and services, define the architecture, assess and implement security controls, and manage changes over time. A CSA can ensure that the cloud solution is secure, compliant, resilient, and trustworthy by following cybersecurity guidance and best practices from providers of cloud computing platforms and other sources.

Different operating systems, especially Linux, Windows, and Mac, are the most common platforms for cloud computing systems and applications. Therefore, a CSA needs to be able to work with them. Cloud solutions that run on different operating systems or interact with them may require a CSA to design, deploy, manage, and troubleshoot them. A CSA may also need various tools and software that are compatible with different operating systems for tasks such as OS imaging and deployment, configuration management, data analytics, and architecture diagramming. Additionally, a CSA may need to understand how each operating system differs in performance, security, scalability, and cost for cloud computing.

Data breaches and attacks can cause severe damage to businesses and customers, so data security is a crucial aspect of cloud computing. Therefore, a CSA needs to know how to store data securely and use cloud database services.

Cloud database services allow a CSA to store, manage, and access data in a scalable and cost-effective way. A CSA can also protect data from unauthorized access by using various techniques and tools, such as encryption, authentication, authorization, backup, recovery, monitoring, and auditing. Additionally, a CSA can classify data, control access levels, track data life cycles, and comply with regulations by implementing data governance policies and processes. A CSA can ensure that the cloud solution meets the data security and performance requirements of the business and customers by knowing how to store data securely and using cloud database services.

Solution architecture design patterns are another area of focus for a CSA. Design patterns help solve common problems that cloud computing exposes. A CSA can use design patterns to build cloud solutions that are reliable, scalable, secure, and cost-effective. Design patterns also make the solution clear to everyone by using commonly accepted terms. One example of a common cloud computing design pattern is the retry pattern, which makes cloud services expect failures and retry failed operations safely. Another example is the gatekeeper pattern, as seen in *Figure 1.5*, which protects applications by using a proxy between clients and an application service:

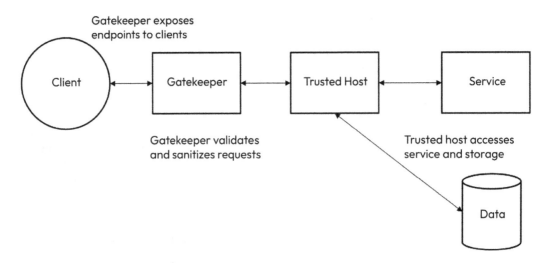

Figure 1.5 – Gatekeeper pattern example

The role of CSA is multi-faceted. The job can be dynamic, even on a day-to-day basis. Many people find this level of variety stimulating and rewarding. However, there are other aspects of the CSA role to explore, some of which are appealing, while others might not be so attractive. Let's explore that next.

Upsides and downsides of being a CSA

While the CSA role is attractive to many, there are potentially both benefits and drawbacks to the career. Variables such as industry, regulations, and pace of innovation for the solutions being designed can all impact the overall job satisfaction of a CSA. Other factors, as described in the following sections, can also determine the overall satisfaction of the role.

High demand and specialized skills for designing and implementing cloud-based solutions give CSAs high earning potential. Various sources report that CSAs in the United States earn an average annual salary of $125,000 to $175,000, which exceeds the national average by far. Experience level, location, industry, and certification are some factors that affect the salary.

Keeping up with the latest trends and technologies in cloud computing gives CSAs continuous learning opportunities. Cloud computing changes and evolves fast and demands constant updating of skills and knowledge. Various sources such as online courses, certification programs, workshops, webinars, blogs, podcasts, and so on help CSAs learn. Working on different projects with different clients and platforms also helps CSAs learn.

Various stakeholders, such as customers, developers, engineers, managers, and so on, interact with CSAs in a collaborative work environment. CSAs understand the customer's needs and goals, design and implement cloud solutions that meet them, communicate and coordinate with other teams involved in the project, and provide ongoing support and improvement. Sharing innovative ideas and learning from others helps CSAs keep up with the latest trends and technologies in cloud computing.

Cloud computing is still growing fast as a platform for software workloads. A report published by Gartner in April 2022 forecasted that worldwide end-user spending on public cloud services would grow in 2023 to roughly $599.8 billion or an approximate increase of 31.5% over 2021 and 17.5% in 2022:

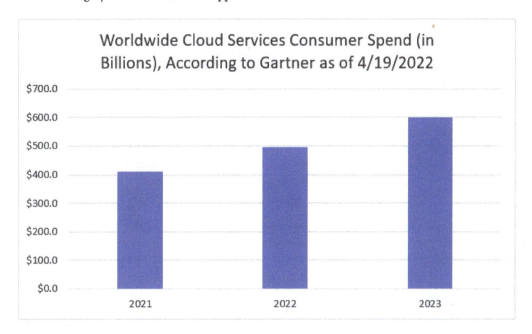

Figure 1.6 – Worldwide cloud spend

Businesses can enjoy many benefits from cloud computing, such as scalability, flexibility, cost efficiency, innovation, and security. A CSA can help them leverage these benefits and achieve their goals more effectively.

Designing and implementing cloud computing solutions that meet the needs and goals of their organizations puts high pressure and responsibility on CSAs. They direct cultural changes required for cloud adoption, build and coordinate cloud architecture, develop a cloud strategy and align the process of adaptation, conduct architectural evaluation, design, and analysis of enterprise-related systems, provide assistance to other IT teams, and ensure compliance with security standards. CSAs also keep up with evolving cloud technologies and best practices and obtain relevant certifications.

Cloud computing is a rapidly evolving field that requires CSAs to update their skills constantly with the latest technologies, best practices, and certifications. CSAs design network, storage, and security solutions that meet business requirements and solve problems. They also have proficiency in basic programming, software development and CI/CD, databases, networking and security skills, modern application architecture skills, and more. Certifications can validate their ability and help them advance their career.

While there are upsides and downsides to being a CSA, it is possible to reduce the downsides. My CSAs focus on specific technology domains, which helps reduce the scope of knowledge required to be effective. This can also help avoid getting burnt out while trying to stay current on all cloud technologies. Let's look at specific technology domains as an option to consider in the role of CSA.

Role-specific cloud technology domains to consider as a career path

Within the cloud computing ecosystem, there are several domains that many CSAs end up specializing in. Data, AI, infrastructure, security, and applications are all areas of specialization in which a CSA can develop expertise. The reason is that the cloud has become vast with service offerings and different environments to provision workloads to. It has become exceedingly difficult to maintain an elevated level of expertise in all aspects of cloud computing.

A CSA focused on data brings expertise in the storage, processing, and security of data to the cloud. Storage can include something as simple as object storage to complex data storage systems such as graph or schema-less repositories. Processing includes data retrieval, transformation, summarization, and analytical opportunities in a secure, reliable way. When considering industries such as healthcare or financial services, security becomes very important when **personally identifiable information (PII)** is being stored. Often, a data CSA has prior experience working with big data solutions, including data lakes.

AI/**machine learning (ML)** on cloud platforms is currently quite popular, with products such as OpenAI's ChatGPT and Google's Bard. This is a very exciting space and is usually a CSA role for someone who has data science or ML expertise. It is also common for a CSA to cover both data and AI/ML as disciplines and provide solutions for both since AI/ML typically requires work with large corpora of data for meaningful results.

For an infrastructure-focused CSA, the domain mostly consists of solution design involving products and services in the IaaS model. They deal with everything from networking within their workload to VM recommendations and configurations. It is also very common to see a focus on network security appliances such as firewalls and proxy servers. This CSA typically comes from a background with an emphasis on enterprise architecture, which has a similar focus on-premises.

The security area of expertise for a CSA is attractive to someone with a cybersecurity or networking security background as most security activities involve securing identities and networks. Application and service-level security configuration can also be included when discussing security as many trust boundaries need to be secured from a CSA perspective.

An application-oriented CSA focuses on distributed design and loosely coupled workloads provisioned to a cloud platform. Because of the nature of the cloud and the potential for individual service failures or faults, this has become the mainstream role of a CSA. It is very common to see a CSA design that includes message queues and service-bus endpoints as a broker between two services so that if a service is down, the other services can gracefully degrade or continue to function.

While it is not required to specialize in a specific area, staying current on all the latest trends in cloud computing in all the different areas of expertise has become a significant challenge. It will require significant dedication to the role in this scenario. As there are many role-specific paths a CSA can take, there are also many tools used by various CSA roles to perform day-to-day responsibilities. Let us look at some common tools of the trade.

Recommended productivity tools for CSAs

Every CSA has a set of tools they prefer to use to design, develop, and deploy cloud computing solutions. There are several options, and each individual product has certain features that draw attention. Regardless of the tool chosen for a specific purpose, there are design tools, development tools, and operational support tools, all required to be successful in the CSA role.

Design tools are typically used to represent logical solution designs. Each cloud provider has a set of icons that represent the various products and services they offer to the CSA. A logical design can be a very useful tool to help a CSA propose a design to the solution stakeholders and get feedback on any areas that may need to be reconsidered.

Lucidchart and Visio are the most common, but there are many options and price points to suit everyone in the CSA role.

Development tools are important as every service or product provisioned might be prototyped as a **proof of concept** (**PoC**) before the development of the solution happens. This can also be referred to as spikes, which are efforts to explore something before committing to it. A very common development tool is VS Code as it provides support for multiple cloud platforms and languages and can run on multiple operating systems.

In a pinch or for a quick development spike, VS Code can also be used to deploy resources to cloud provider platforms, but for the actual development of a product solution, the best way to automate the provisioning of cloud resources is via the CI/CD pipeline.

Networking tools are extremely important to a CSA as they help understand and configure network connectivity, which protocols to use, and why a particular network path may be blocked. There are many options to choose from, but please proceed with caution when using a network sniffing tool such as Wireshark. Many IT organizations discourage the use of these products, and your PC/laptop might get flagged and create alerts when running. Make sure that if you use these tools, IT and security people are aware of the usage and allow it.

If installation of tools is not allowed, cloud providers typically offer a network monitoring tool such as Azure's Network Watcher. These services still typically require a certain user role for access.

One tool a CSA should be proficient in, regardless of any others, is the **command-line interface** (**CLI**). While the cloud provider's portal provides an educational aspect by providing visual representations of how to deploy, configure, and delete resources in the cloud, the CLI is for a user who has intermediate-level experience. By using the CLI combined with script automation, the process of interacting with resources in the cloud can be sped up, thus allowing the CSA to reduce the **time to value** (**TTV**) of using cloud services and products. Instead of launching the portal and navigating around, the CLI can be executed via a PowerShell console, a Bash console, and so on.

Finally, **cloud service provider** (**CSP**) tools help integrate, manage, monitor, and optimize cloud services in private/public/hybrid cloud space, such as AWS CloudFormation, Azure Resource Manager, Google Cloud Deployment Manager, and so on. Without operational support, the cloud becomes a black box with limited visibility into diagnostic logs, elasticity events, service outage alerts, and many more. When multiple products are combined, a comprehensive view can be achieved to proactively support workloads running on a cloud platform, as seen in *Figure 1.7*:

Figure 1.7 – AWS CloudWatch example

The preceding screenshot is a great example of monitoring capabilities provided by AWS natively, necessary to aid CSAs in monitoring cloud solutions.

We now have a good understanding of the role of CSA.

Summary

In summary, we covered the role of CSA by starting with a brief history of cloud computing and the enabling capabilities that were developed to run software and services on a platform provided by a cloud provider. Many primitive constructs necessary to enable cloud infrastructure were developed back as long ago as the 1950s. Today, cloud computing continues to evolve and provide new features at a rapid pace.

Next, we explored some common cloud capabilities that a CSA needs to have a deep understanding of to be successful. Whether building an IaaS or a PaaS solution or leveraging a SaaS product, a CSA needs to understand how they fit together. Hybrid cloud solutions can contain edge computing and on-premises services or data and add complexity to a solution design. To stay consistent in the adoption and continued usage of cloud computing, a CSA should pay close attention to the CAF to start and apply the WAF to each solution to ensure best practices and industry standards are followed.

Once we finished with the base foundation of technology for the role of CSA, we then moved on to the actual role of CSA. The role requires a certain skill set and abilities. Some are universal and some are specific to a domain, but there are also some basic expectations of a CSA. Usually, the role is continuously refined as experience is gained and wisdom achieved through years of work and solutions' successes and failures.

After the introduction to the role of CSA, the reality of the role was presented, and both the benefits and liabilities of the role were discussed. The role is in demand and compensation is decent, but it is common for long hours and stress to be associated with cloud computing solutions being created.

Finally, we talked about some common tools that are used in the daily activities of a CSA. Each phase of solution creation has a specific type of tool used, from diagramming to developing to monitoring a solution when it is finally released into production. There are many options to choose from, and each has pluses and minuses.

It should now be clear that designing a solution architecture for cloud computing necessitates the dedicated role of CSA. As a CSA, many areas of cloud technology domains require attention. Because of this, in the next chapter, we will explore these domains in more detail as areas of dedication for a CSA.

2

Types of Cloud Solution Architect Roles

In *Chapter 1, Understanding the Responsibilities of a Cloud Solution Architect*, we discovered what the role of a CSA entails and how the role has evolved. Through this learning, we came to understand that there are different areas of specialization to consider. Within each area of expertise, there are some overlaps of responsibilities, but each has a unique domain and set of concerns to focus on.

Because of the number of cloud providers services, products, and configuration options, CSAs tend to gravitate toward areas of expertise; it is not uncommon to see a CSA with a specific discipline preceding the title of *Cloud Solution Architect*. Usually, the disciplines will be infrastructure, application, data, **artificial intelligence** (**AI**) and/or **machine learning** (**ML**), and security.

You don't require specialization to be an effective CSA, but the chances of a successful career go up when the amount of understanding is scoped to specific domains. Staying current with all cloud providers products and services across all technology domains warrants a considerable amount of time to be able to design effectively across all pillars of the **Well-Architected Framework** (**WAF**), also mentioned in *Chapter 1, Understanding the Responsibilities of a Cloud Solution Architect*.

In this chapter, we will continue to explore the role of a CSA by examining the areas of expertise in which a CSA can specialize. By understanding these areas and what types of responsibilities each one entails, it should become clearer what the path to being a successful CSA can look like.

This chapter will describe each discipline in greater detail and provide role expectations to help you determine if it is a discipline you wish to pursue as an aspiring CSA. For each area of expertise, the general role's responsibilities, available certifications, and samples of design patterns for solution architecture will be provided. A baseline expectation across all CSA areas of expertise will also be provided.

In this chapter, we will explore the following areas that a prospective CSA should consider:

- All CSAs
- Infrastructure CSA
- Application CSA
- Data CSA
- AI/ML CSA
- Security CSA

All CSAs

A CSA role generally requires a degree in computer science, computer engineering, information technology, or even electrical engineering to a lesser extent. Another approach would be to gain hands-on experience along the way; this would be the rough equivalent of the degrees mentioned previously. **Amazon Web Services (AWS)**, Microsoft Azure, and Google Cloud are the most sought-after cloud computing platforms that are leveraged by companies looking for an experienced CSA, but it is not uncommon to see open positions requiring experience with Alibaba, IBM Cloud, or Oracle Cloud as well. Regardless of the cloud provider platform, experience with infrastructure automation tools is typically listed in job postings for a CSA as knowledge about these tools is necessary to perform **Infrastructure as Code (IaC)** automation.

The required logical infrastructure knowledge includes networking protocols such as TCP/IP/UDP, HTTP/HTTPS/MQTT/AMPQ, DNS, and VPN since these are the most common protocols available and used on a cloud provider platform. VMware and Hyper-V and containerization technologies such as Docker and Kubernetes are great technologies to become intimately familiar with as they help a CSA understand how the underpinnings of a cloud platform work and where the CSA's responsibility lies for designing solutions. The following figure depicts who is responsible for the technology under which a model will be deployed and where most CSAs will generally focus time to design solution architectures:

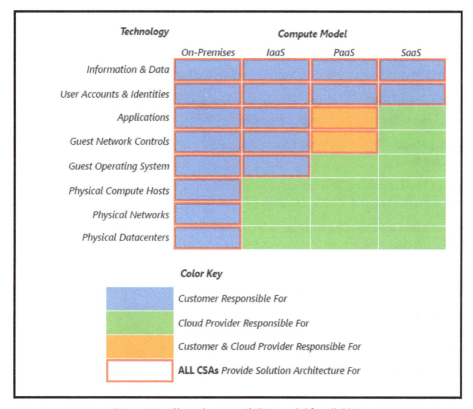

Figure 2.1 – Shared responsibility model for all CSAs

Also, familiarity with scripting languages such as Python, Bash, and PowerShell is expected and will likely be used extensively to complement IaC, DevSecOps, and configuration management on all cloud providers platforms. Knowledge of security best practices for cloud infrastructure is extremely important due to the multitenant nature of cloud computing in general.

To demonstrate competency in the disciplines mentioned previously, cloud providers offer professional certifications for CSAs. For example, Google Cloud's *Professional Cloud Architect* certification exam measures your ability to design, manage, and provision a cloud solution infrastructure. The exam also covers security and compliance design considerations.

Similarly, Microsoft Azure's *Solutions Architect* certification requires subject matter expertise in designing cloud and hybrid solutions that run on Microsoft Azure, including compute, network, storage, monitor, and security.

AWS also offers *Certified Solutions Architect – Associate Certification*, which is a great starting point on the AWS certification path for individuals who have experience in AWS technology; strong on-premises IT experience and understanding of mapping on-premises to the cloud; and experience working in other cloud services.

Also, as part of the demonstration of competency within cloud disciplines, CSAs should know about different software and infrastructure design patterns as these can help them create cloud solutions that support architecture requirements such as resiliency, durability, high availability, scalability, and security. Some of these patterns are ubiquitous across CSA areas of specialization and include the following:

- **Bulkhead pattern**: This pattern involves isolating elements in a cloud solution architecture into pools so that if one pool fails, others can continue to function

- **Retry pattern**: This pattern involves retrying connections automatically in the event of a transient failure

- **Circuit breaker pattern**: This pattern detects platform or service failures and temporarily stops communication to unavailable resources

- **Queue-based load leveling pattern**: This pattern allows solutions to scale horizontally across multiple service instances so that they can scale out and handle the load on the system

- **Throttling pattern**: This pattern is used to control the rate of requests to a service to ensure that the rate of data flow can be digested by a service

Many more design patterns target cloud platforms, in addition to those mentioned here. Most cloud providers also provide a catalog of cloud design patterns that address specific challenges in distributed systems, such as availability, high availability, operational excellence, resiliency, performance, and security. Now that we understand common focus areas of solution architectures, let's explore specific domains of CSA roles and what should be considered.

Infrastructure CSA

An infrastructure CSA generally supervises an organization's cloud computing ecosystem at the infrastructure, networking, storage, and virtual machine levels. This includes working with other domain-specific CSAs for cloud management and monitoring. As opposed to all CSA roles, the infrastructure role focuses on a subset of technologies in the shared responsibility model, as depicted in *Figure 2.2*:

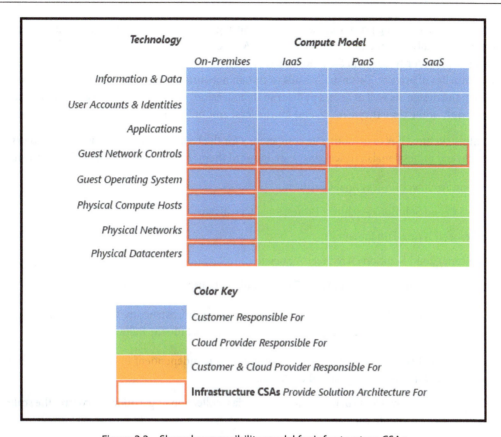

Figure 2.2 – Shared responsibility model for infrastructure CSAs

Infrastructure CSAs typically design and maintain the infrastructure of solution architectures and their deployments in a cloud-based environment, as well as the configuration of products and services. This role often provides design and configuration guidance for a solution's infrastructure, operating environment, applications, and services as well.

In addition to design requirements, an infrastructure CSA can also be responsible for leading cultural changes for cloud adoption. This is due to the nature of overlap between on-premises and cloud platforms from an enterprise architecture perspective. An infrastructure CSA tends to help bridge the gap between how technology is implemented on-premises and how services are consumed on a cloud platform.

Evaluating and maintaining existing solution architectures is another important aspect of the infrastructure CSA's primary duties. As cloud platforms continue to evolve, existing services are enhanced, new services are released, and some legacy services will eventually become obsolete. Keeping an organization's solution architectures updated is important to take full advantage of a cloud platform and avoid potential security issues that may be discovered over time.

Monitoring and maintaining privacy in the cloud by ensuring that identity, data, assets, and applications are secure is typically a joint effort with a security CSA. The infrastructure CSA will provide a logical design, while the security CSA will likely address requirements to understand what steps must be taken to avoid breaches of privacy. This usually leads to certain network appliances, such as firewalls, being included in the design, as well as access policies so that identities can only have access to the services they need, only at the time they need it, and for the least amount of time required to do their jobs.

For an infrastructure CSA to demonstrate competency for the responsibilities mentioned previously, there are several professional certifications geared toward them. Some of them include the following:

- Cloud Architect Professional Certificate

- AWS Cloud Solutions Architect Professional Certificate

- Microsoft Azure Fundamentals

- Tencent Cloud Solutions Architect Associate

- **Information Technology (IT)** and Cloud Fundamentals Specialization by IBM

Again, as part of the ability to demonstrate competency as an infrastructure CSA, different design patterns become areas of focus and expertise. These patterns include the following

- **Deployment stamps**: The ability to provision multiple independent instances of a collection of services for scale or geopolitical concerns.

- **Sharding**: This involves providing data storage via a collection of partitions to control the scale and scope of access to the data.

- **Strangler fig**: This involves slowly migrating a solution by swapping out legacy components with new cloud-native products and services over time.

- **Valet key**: This involves providing a user or service with a key that grants restricted access to a product or service for a limited amount of time.

- **Geodes**: This involves provisioning a pool of resources or services into a specific geo-location that can take requests from any other location.

These design patterns, among others, are useful for building reliable, scalable, and secure applications in the cloud. As mentioned previously, cloud providers will also provide specific design patterns relating to their platforms as the need arises. Now that we have explored the infrastructure domain of CSA areas of expertise, let's move on to the application CSA, which focuses on technologies that are typically enabled by solution architectures and designed in collaboration with the infrastructure CSA.

Application CSA

An application CSA works with developers to ensure that applications are designed according to cloud architecture principles and best practices, as well as meet the requirements of the various solution stakeholders. Because of the services and products that are leveraged, this role tends to focus on the application code and configuration, as well as some network controls, depending on which compute model is used. This is illustrated in *Figure 2.3*:

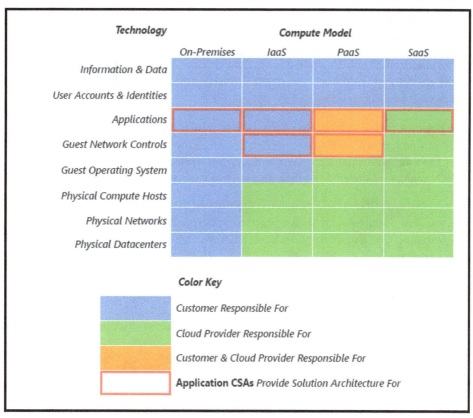

Figure 2.3 – Shared responsibility model for application CSAs

Application CSAs focus on how technologies, products, and services can be used to solve business problems. It is very common for solution architectures to include cloud-native and PaaS services as part of the solution. These designs complement the underpinnings provided by the infrastructure CSA and typically involve collaboration between the CSAs.

Also, within the products and services, an application CSA needs to help decide what framework, platform, or technical stack should be used to create a solution. Ideally, this is influenced in large part by the business requirements and non-functional requirements provided by stakeholders. How the solution will interact with other systems or solutions will also be a contributing factor.

Finally, an application CSA will assess solution architectures across common pillars of software quality:

- **Reliability**: They will ensure that an application architecture will not prohibit the solution from being available

- **Security**: They will confirm that appropriate authentication and authorization are in place for users, services, and products that interact within the solution architecture and external interactions with the solution

- **Cost optimization**: They will provide recommendations to avoid overprovisioning application-level resources, which can drive costs up

- **Performance efficiency**: They will drive performance optimizations by allowing concepts such as the elasticity of cloud resources to enable scalability and throughput and asynchronous interactions to avoid blocking

Again, one potential metric of competency for the responsibilities mentioned here is certifications. There are several professional certifications geared toward an application CSA. Some of them include AWS's *Certified Solution Architect*, the *Professional Cloud Architect* certification from Google GCP, and the *Azure Solutions Architect Expert* certification from Microsoft.

For a well-rounded application CSA, common design patterns that are used in solution design include anti-corruption layer, **Command Query Responsibility Segregation** (**CQRS**), sidecar, leader election, and gateway routing. The anti-corruption layer design pattern uses an adapter to allow disparate subsystems to communicate.

CQRS is a common pattern that's used to separate read and write operations to grant least common access to users and other solutions.

The sidecar pattern is used to provide common functionality to a variety of services by way of isolation and encapsulation. This pattern is a very common approach in container orchestration technologies to share common functionality across multiple containers. Next, the leader election pattern is very common in distributed systems where nominating one instance, out of many, to manage other instances is required.

Finally, the gateway routing pattern demonstrates the ability to enable multiple requests to multiple services by a single source or endpoint. This pattern is common in control plane operations on cloud platforms. As it is common for an application CSA to work with infrastructure CSAs, it is also common for both roles to collaborate with a data CSA. Without data, both infrastructure and application solution architectures provide limited value as data is moved back and forth on the infrastructure and used/presented in the application. So, let's explore the data CSA role.

Data CSA

A data CSA is responsible for designing and implementing cloud-based data solutions using traditional tools, as well as cloud-native capabilities. When cloud computing was first presented to users, most data solutions were traditional relational database storage solutions or object storage services. Today, a data CSA might work with NoSQL databases, data lakes, and data exploration tools in addition to the early services and products. In the shared responsibility model, the data CSA will focus on information and data, as well as application integration, as indicated in *Figure 2.4*:

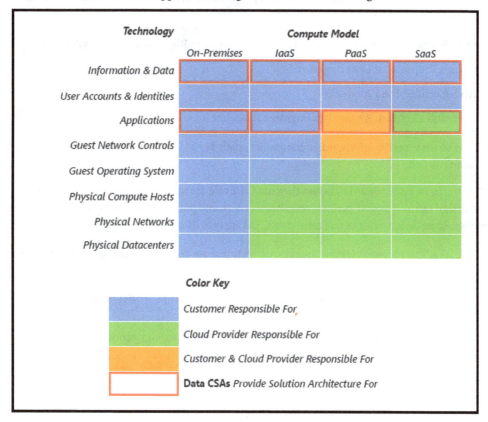

Figure 2.4 – Shared responsibility model for data CSAs

Not only will a data CSA work with data services and products, but their responsibilities also include analyzing, planning, and defining data architecture frameworks, including security, reference data, metadata, and master data.

Most solution architectures on cloud platforms involve some type of data storage and retrieval, so data CSAs often collaborate with other teams and CSAs within the organization to devise and implement data strategies, build models, and assess shareholder needs and goals for a more comprehensive solution architecture.

Data CSAs also have a hand in managing frontend platforms, servers, storage, delivery, and networks required to manage cloud storage. This also includes monitoring data services and products so that they have a feedback loop for future optimizations and cost savings.

Finally, the last responsibility that falls within the role of the data CSA is data classification and categorization. *Classification* refers to the level of compliance concerns associated with the data, while *categorization* refers to the impact exfiltrating private data has on a business.

Regarding these responsibilities, there are several professional certifications for a data CSA. Some of them include the following:

- **Data Science Council of America (DASCA) Associate Big Data Engineer (ABDE)**
- Google Professional Data Engineer
- AWS Certified Data Analytics
- Microsoft Certified: Azure Data Engineer Associate

In addition to these certifications, other companies, such as IBM and Oracle, have provider-specific certifications as well.

Design patterns targeted toward data and the data CSA role are just as important as other roles. Poor solution design can lead to slow performance, higher costs, and potential security issues in the data area of expertise. Some design patterns that most data CSAs apply to data solution architectures are as follows:

- *Indexing*: This involves creating indexes on fields that are commonly used as filter criteria when running a query against the data
- *Sharding*: This involves creating horizontal/row-level partitions to store that data for performance gains
- *Cache-aside*: This involves storing data in a cache from a storage repository on demand for quick reads and/or writes of the data

  These design patterns help facilitate storage and the operations that are performed against data, as well as the scalability of the data usage. This is very important to an AI/ML CSA, where data scale and access are critical to timely results.

Next, we'll explore the AI/ML CSA role to see what makes this role unique.

AI/ ML CSA

As the name suggests, an AI/ML CSA is responsible for designing and implementing cloud-based AI/ML solutions. Close collaboration with data scientists and data CSAs happens frequently to ensure that AI/ML solutions are designed according to cloud data architecture principles and best practices within the AI/ML area of expertise. Solution architectures need to be scalable, secure, and highly available. This often requires hybrid or burstable workloads, as defined in *Chapter 1, Understanding the Responsibilities of a Cloud Solution Architect*. Because of the additional complexity, infrastructure CSAs are commonly consulted to ensure established communication routes and security measures are built into the architecture between on-premises and cloud platforms.

As shown in *Figure 2.5*, the AI/ML CSA provides solution architectures in technology areas that are identical to those the data CSA provides. Because of this overlap, it is very common for there to be a CSA role that combines both areas of expertise:

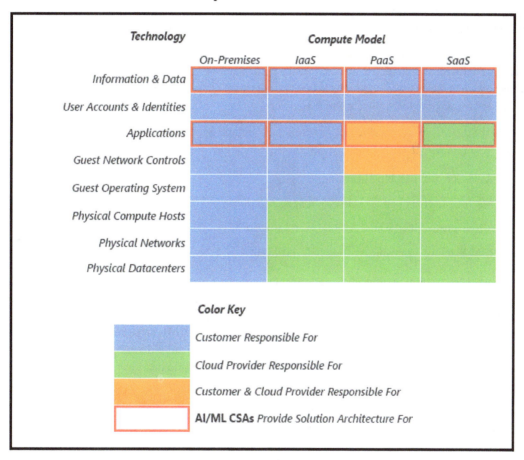

Figure 2.5 – Shared responsibility model for AI/ML CSAs

In the preceding figure, we can see that an AI/ML CSA works primarily with information and data technologies while providing data actions, such as ML algorithms, usually in an application layer.

Data and technology pipelines are another common area of interest for an AI/ML CSA. AI/ML CSAs generally drive full life cycle management for envisioning, building, deploying, and operationalizing an end-to-end ML and AI pipeline. A robust enterprise-wide pipeline architecture for AI/ML helps drive infrastructure for applications, databases, and computer networks. The ability to focus on finding models that accurately capture the intricate relationships in the data adds significant productivity gains when infrastructure-level capabilities can be handled by the cloud platform provider. This, in turn, leads to business value being created through accurate predictions.

Architecting systems for **machine learning operations** (**MLOps**) generally falls under the responsibility of the AI/ML CSA, in addition to the tasks mentioned previously. ML engineers benefit from significant productivity gains when MLOps is implemented to optimize the process of creating production-quality ML models. To have maximum impact on productivity, an AI/ML CSA will also provide solutions for managing and monitoring pipelines and production workloads relating to AI and ML.

Finally, as part of continuous solution life cycle maturity, the post-deployment of AI and ML workloads includes continuous feedback loops to analyze the performance of AI/ML models in online and offline scenarios, which helps correspond solutions to the corporate environment, and develop solutions that will be easily integrated into the corporate structure.

Within the AI/ML space, specific certifications exist and are commonly a requirement by potential employers of an AI/ML CSA. The most common certifications are as follows:

- AWS Certified Machine Learning
- Machine Learning on Google Cloud Specialization
- Microsoft Certified Azure AI Engineer Associate
- IBM Machine Learning Professional Certificate

Since these certifications are specific to various cloud providers platforms, universities will sometimes offer cloud certifications that aren't specific to a cloud computing platform providers services or products. A great example is Cornell University. Cornell offers an ML certificate that targets developers, engineers, and managers who are interested in ML and data science. This can be beneficial to someone who wants to understand more general academic constructs instead of learning product-specific implementations for topics such as building ML algorithms. Each cloud provider may have a different way of creating and deploying algorithms that are specific to their products.

Both with experience and through the certification process, common models and design patterns emerge for an AI/ML CSA. While design patterns do exist within the role of the AI/ML CSA, they tend to be less common than models that are used for implementing algorithms. As far as traditional design patterns are concerned, the following common patterns are used by an AI/ML CSA:

- **Sharding**: As mentioned previously, sharding refers to creating horizontal/row-level partitions for storing data for performance gains
- **Valet key**: The practice of providing a key or token that's used to gain access to resources or sensitive data for a specific amount of time
- **Pipes and filters**: This involves connecting reusable subtasks into a pipeline process for tasks such as processing data or training a data model

- **Leader election**: As mentioned previously, this pattern is common to **high-performance compute (HPC)** workloads for performing tasks such as scheduling jobs, performing health checks, and distributing workloads across peer nodes in a cluster

So far, we have looked at design patterns that are specific to a discipline area of the CSA role. We have also observed that collaboration tends to happen across disciplines with some common design patterns. The next role we will discuss is the security CSA. This role is the most likely to collaborate across many – if not all – roles as security is critical in every technology across every deployment model.

Security CSA

Security CSAs are responsible for building, designing, deploying, and monitoring security aspects of solution architecture for cloud-based computing and data storage systems. Because security crosscuts every area of expertise of cloud computing, as indicated in *Figure 2.6*, a security CSA is the most likely to collaborate with the other CSA disciplines. Also, bad actors are always inventing new ways to thwart security controls, so a security CSA is constantly evolving in thinking and exploring new tools and technologies to secure resources:

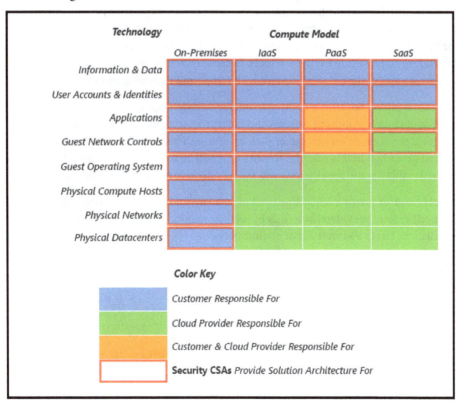

Figure 2.6 – Shared responsibility model for security CSAs

The preceding figure shows that a security CSA is responsible for all technologies in all the deployment models not owned exclusively by the cloud provider. This requires collaboration and co-designing with the other disciplines to ensure CSAs are secure across all products and services that are used.

A security CSA may also be involved in the act of **penetration testing (pen testing)** existing cloud computing security systems. Based on the results of the tests, the security CSA may add firewalls, improve network security, and encrypt data to secure the system further. This iterative, evolving design approach helps the enterprise reduce attacks on cloud service data storage, create preventative features, and implement corrective controls when breaches do occur.

Not only will a security CSA create a security posture in front of cloud products and services, but concepts such as zero-trust, least-privilege access, and identity life cycle management also play a crucial role in the day-to-day operations of a security CSA. Identity management and least-privilege access are crucial in blocking bad actors from gaining access to a cloud workload. Regular access reviews by a security CSA can help remove identities that no longer need access to a given resource and limit the type of access an individual or service has to a cloud resource. This helps avoid an escalation of privilege scenario and limits the blast radius on cloud resources, should an identity get spoofed or compromised.

Many cloud platform providers offer comprehensive tools and services to help mitigate attacks and vulnerabilities on a cloud computing product or service. As mentioned previously, threats and bad actors are constantly looking for new and novel ways to penetrate defenses, and most platform providers invest heavily in creating and evolving mitigation tools. Because of this evolution, the security CSA spends a considerable amount of time staying current with trends and technologies in the security domain.

A security CSA typically requires a computer-related college degree or equivalent experience, an understanding of cloud computing systems and enterprise security, and professional certification. Security CSAs generally start on this career path by earning a bachelor's degree in computer science or computer engineering. In this role, the security CSA will be responsible for defending the security of cloud-based platforms and applications and taking offensive measures as needed.

To stay current and/or provide a baseline level of security understanding, many certifications are offered by specific cloud providers, as well as by security vendors and organizations with no specific provider affiliation. Here's a sample list of certifications:

- AWS Solutions Architect – Associate
- Microsoft Certified: Azure Security Engineer Associate
- IBM Certified Technical Advocate - Cloud v3
- Cloud Security Alliance: **Certificate of Cloud Security Knowledge (CCSK)**
- CISSP: Certified Information Systems Security Professional

As indicated in previous disciplines, design patterns are common reference tools for the security CSA as well. These patterns include the following:

- **Federated identity pattern**: A very common pattern in cloud workloads, this pattern allows the authentication of an identity to be handled by an external identity provider

- **Gatekeeper pattern**: This pattern provides a broker to directly control access to a resource or service

- **Valet key**: As mentioned previously, this pattern is the practice of providing a key or token that's used to gain access to resources or sensitive data for a specific amount of time

The security CSA has architecture design responsibilities that span all technologies and deployment models in cloud computing. They are responsible for security at all levels of the computing stack in which they have exclusive or shared responsibilities, as described in *Figure 2.6*. There are design patterns at their disposal to ensure they are following best practices, but collaboration with other CSA disciplines is critical to ensuring all products and services that are deployed are not vulnerable to security breaches.

Summary

As part of understanding the role that a CSA plays, this chapter has been important in learning which technical areas should be learned when selecting a CSA domain to pursue. While there are multiple areas of expertise for a CSA to specialize in, there are some universal truths that apply to all disciplines across education, certifications, and design patterns that will apply to the CSA role. In other cases, specific certifications can be applied to each role, and design patterns exist to help create reliable, secure, and scalable solutions, regardless of whether the CSA specializes in infrastructure, applications, data, AI/ML, or security.

Moving forward, in Chapter 3, *Education Paths to the Cloud Solution Architect Role*, we will be exploring areas you should consider when pursuing a CSA role, including who in your professional network might be able to provide guidance in securing a CSA role, and what might be expected of you from a job responsibilities perspective.

Part 2: Pursuing the Role

This part considers how to get ready for your career as a cloud solution architect – from education to landing a job, we cover the options and considerations to account for when skilling up and preparing for your job hunt.

This part has the following chapters:

- *Chapter 3, Education Paths to the Cloud Solution Architect Role*
- *Chapter 4, Getting Real Experience*
- *Chapter 5, Closing In on Opportunities*

3

Education Paths to the Cloud Solution Architect Role

In previous chapters, we described the role of the **Cloud Solution Architect** (**CSA**) and the responsibilities that come with the role. In this chapter, we will explore educational options in depth to understand what career paths are available to qualify for the role of CSA. By the end of this chapter, the education paths to become a CSA will be clear and the options for certification paths will be examined to provide clarity regarding the multiple paths to successfully pursue the career of a CSA.

The role of a CSA is an important one in today's technology-driven world. It requires a deep understanding of cloud computing concepts, architectures, and services, as well as effective communication, collaboration, and leadership skills. A CSA is responsible for designing and implementing cloud-based solutions that meet the business needs of an organization while ensuring security, scalability, reliability, and cost-effectiveness.

To become a CSA, one needs to have a solid educational background in computer science, information technology, or a related field. There are many educational options available for aspiring CSAs, such as online courses, bootcamps, degree programs, and certifications. These educational options can help one gain the necessary knowledge and skills to succeed in this field.

One can also pursue various paths for certain disciplines to become a CSA. For example, one can specialize in cloud security, cloud networking, cloud storage, cloud databases, or cloud development. Each path requires different skills and knowledge, but it all leads to the same goal of becoming a successful CSA.

Certifications are also an important part of becoming a CSA. They demonstrate one's expertise and credibility in specific areas of cloud computing and can help one stand out from other candidates in the job market.

In this chapter, the following topics will be covered:

- Picking a cloud provider or provider agnostic
- College degrees to land a role as a CSA
- CSA certifications
- Self-paced learning

These three sections should provide enough insight for a potential CSA to understand what education options are available for CSA role education and how the different paths may vary.

Technical requirements

This chapter has very basic technical requirements. All that is needed is access to a library or a device with internet access. Most of the content is provided as a jumping-off point for further research if desired or as a reference to online education and/or certification platforms.

Picking a cloud provider or provider agnostic

Focusing on a specific cloud computing platform provider such as Amazon, Microsoft, or Google versus focusing on general cloud computing concepts has its pros and cons in the pursuit of a role as a CSA.

Concentrating on a specific cloud computing platform provider can help you gain in-depth knowledge of that platform and become an expert in it. This can be beneficial if you are looking for a job that requires expertise in that specific platform. However, it may limit your career opportunities as you may not be able to work with other platforms.

On the other hand, focusing on general cloud computing concepts can help you gain knowledge of multiple platforms and make you more versatile. This can be beneficial if you are looking for a job that requires knowledge of multiple platforms. However, it may not make you an expert in any specific platform.

It is also possible that the starting goal might be to remain cloud agnostic, but a job might require in-depth knowledge of a specific cloud provider platform. The key is to be flexible and adjust over time to the requirements of the role for a specific employer.

It is important to note that either approach has advantages and disadvantages, and the choice ultimately depends on one's career goals and interests. If one is interested in working for a specific cloud computing platform provider or wants to specialize in a particular area of cloud computing, then focusing on that platform or area may be the best option. However, if one is interested in working with multiple platforms or wants to gain a broad understanding of cloud computing concepts, then focusing on general cloud computing concepts may be the way to go.

Another factor to consider is the job market. Some cloud computing platform providers may have more job opportunities than others, depending on their market share and customer base. For example, **Amazon Web Services (AWS)** is currently the market leader in cloud computing, followed by **Microsoft Azure** and **Google Cloud Platform (GCP)**. Therefore, focusing on AWS may provide more job opportunities than focusing on GCP or other providers.

However, it is important to keep in mind that the cloud computing market is constantly evolving, and new providers may emerge as major players in the future. Therefore, it is important to stay up to date with the latest trends and developments in the industry.

Whether to focus on a specific cloud computing platform provider or general cloud computing concepts as a CSA depends on one's career goals and interests. Both approaches have their advantages and disadvantages, and the choice should be made based on careful consideration of these factors. Regardless of which approach one chooses, continuous learning and staying up to date with the latest trends and developments in the industry are essential for success as a CSA.

College degrees to land a role as a CSA

Most job postings for CSA roles prefer a traditional two/four-year degree or equivalent experience. A technical background is necessary, commonly paired with a technical degree. A degree in computer science/programming provides a baseline understanding to design and deploy solutions but will likely be environmentally agnostic. Additional learning and/or experience is needed because cloud platforms have some unique considerations, as mentioned in previous chapters.

Typically, a CSA will not be hired directly out of college without a complimentary set of credentials such as certifications or experience. It is very common for a recent college graduate to enter the workforce as an engineer with the goal of becoming a CSA over time.

Entering the workforce as a software engineer usually is predicated on the successful completion of a two- or four-year degree focusing on computer science, management information systems, or other closely related degrees. Along with the degree, internship experience is very common and can provide a differentiator when two candidates applying for the same CSA role have similar backgrounds. In addition to the time commitment for the degree, there is also the learning environment to consider. Some people may learn better in a traditional, in-person environment while others may thrive in an online, virtual type of setting. In the case where a degree is not required, attaining a degree is still an option, with many organizations offering some form of tuition reimbursement to help offset the costs of education, usually after a period of time as an employee.

Online degree options for aspiring CSAs

There are many accredited online colleges and universities that offer a wide range of computer science and related programs. Here are some of the best accredited online colleges and universities of 2023 according to `accreditedschoolsonline.org`:

- **Southern New Hampshire University**: This university offers over 200 online programs and is accredited by the New England Commission of Higher Education

- **University of Florida**: This university offers over 200 online programs and is accredited by the Southern Association of Colleges and Schools Commission on Colleges

- **Arizona State University**: This university offers over 200 online programs and is accredited by the Higher Learning Commission

- **University of Central Florida**: This university offers over 100 online programs and is accredited by the Southern Association of Colleges and Schools Commission on Colleges

- **University of Illinois at Urbana-Champaign**: This university offers over 80 online programs and is accredited by the Higher Learning Commission

You can also check out OnlineU's (`https://www.onlineu.com/online-schools`) comprehensive list of accredited online schools that cover over 40,367 fully online degrees at the associate, bachelor's, master's, doctoral, and certificate levels.

In addition to traditional college educational paths to land CSA roles, certifications can also play a large part in landing a CSA role. Let us now look at the different cloud provider and provider agnostic programs and how they can help land a role as a CSA.

CSA certifications

Major cloud computing providers provide certification paths for current and aspiring CSAs. They tend to update the exams for the certifications on an annual basis, so recertifying is very common to stay current with CSA certification credentials. Like collegiate degrees, learning can be online and self-paced or can happen in a classroom type of setting. This flexibility enables people with different learning styles and paces to be equally successful. Also, after successfully achieving a certification, a badge is earned and independently verified. This allows a CSA to display the badges on social media sites associated with their profile or resume. An example of the certification badges can be seen in the following figure:

Figure 3.1 – Cloud provider certification badges

Figure 3.1 provides examples of certification badges from each major cloud provider that can be displayed on social media profiles, professional networking sites, and resumes.

The following certification paths are available to any person looking to extend their knowledge of cloud computing. There are many providers that provide certification opportunities, but the three major providers have the most adoption and visibility in the cloud computing community of technical experts. Let us now look at the major cloud providers: Microsoft, Amazon, and Google, and explore their specific certification options.

Microsoft Azure certifications

Microsoft Azure offers diverse types of certifications for distinct roles. These certifications are divided into three levels: Fundamental level, Associate level, and Expert level. Each level builds on the previous level to demonstrate a deeper and more thorough understanding of the cloud computing products and services provided by the Microsoft Azure platform.

Here are some of the certification options available for Microsoft Azure along with their descriptions:

- **Azure Fundamentals**: This certification validates your basic, foundational understanding of Microsoft Azure products and services. Generally, the physical infrastructure is explored and how the platform achieves high availability, securing of services, and geo-political locations of the regional data centers are covered. Practice exams are available to increase the likelihood of passing the exam before scheduling it.

- **Azure Administrator Associate**: This certification is optimized to demonstrate skills and knowledge targeting individuals responsible for implementing security controls, managing enterprise identity and access, and protecting data, applications, and networks in cloud and hybrid environments. Concepts such as command-line interaction and governance are covered in addition to achieving outcomes such as zero-trust and least-privilege access.

- **Azure Developer Associate**: This is a certification designed for developers who have experience building cloud applications and services on the Microsoft Azure platform. Candidates should have experience with Azure SDKs, APIs, data storage options, and app authentication and authorization.

- **Azure Security Engineer Associate**: This is a certification that demonstrates the ability to implement, manage, and monitor security for resources, multi-cloud, and hybrid environments as part of the Microsoft Azure platform. This specific certification focuses on topics such as identity and access management, infrastructure networking, cloud computing services, storage, and databases from a security perspective.

- **Azure AI Engineer Associate**: This certification is designed for individuals who use Microsoft Azure's AI Cognitive Services product, machine learning algorithms, and knowledge mining patterns to architect and implement workloads based on Microsoft Azure's AI products and services.

- **Azure Data Engineer Associate**: Individuals who own the creation and delivery of the management, monitoring, and security of data using Azure data services to fulfill business needs can earn this certification. This certification confirms their expertise in these areas.

- **Azure Solutions Architect Expert**: This certification is designed for professionals who have advanced experience and knowledge of IT operations and Azure features. Candidates should be able to design solutions that run on Azure using several Azure products and services as part of the solution.

Helpful tips to become Microsoft Azure certified

As part of the Microsoft Azure certification process, Microsoft provides some tips on how to approach the certification exams. You can find the tips in the following list:

- **Get training and develop relevant skills**: This is essential for becoming certified. This typically includes attending a Microsoft Azure Virtual Training Day class or signing up for an instructor-led training event.

- **Meet the prerequisites for each level**: Meeting the prerequisites for each level before attempting the certification exam will aid in the successful completion of the certification exams. This includes understanding the diverse types of Azure certifications available and choosing the one that best fits your career goals.

- **Pass the certification exam**: Passing the certification exam after developing the relevant skills and meeting the prerequisites for each level is essential for becoming Azure certified.

- **Choose the right Azure exam and certification**: Choosing the right Azure exam and certification based on your career goals is important. This includes starting with a fundamentals-level exam related to your career if you are new to Azure.

- **Know the exam content and read about what is measured**: Knowing the exam content and reading about what is measured before taking the certification exam is important. This includes understanding what skills are measured in each certification exam.

- **Leverage a sandbox environment for hands-on experience**: Leveraging development subscriptions for hands-on experience is an effective way to get practical experience with Azure. This includes setting up test environments and experimenting with different Azure services.

- **Take practice exams**: Taking practice exams is an effective way to help you prepare for the certification exam. This includes using resources such as Microsoft Learn or other online training videos.

- **Book your exam and prepare**: Booking your exam and preparing accordingly after preparing for the certification exam is crucial for success. This includes setting goals, creating a study schedule, and identifying resources such as books, PDFs, and online training videos.

Now that we have covered the Microsoft Azure certifications, let us now look at Amazon's AWS Cloud platform certifications.

Amazon AWS certifications

AWS offers diverse types of certifications for distinct roles. These certifications are divided into four levels: Foundational level, Associate level, Professional level, and Specialty level.

Here are some of the certification options available for Amazon AWS along with their descriptions:

- **AWS Certified Cloud Practitioner**: This certification validates your overall understanding of the AWS Cloud. It covers the basic concepts and terminology of the AWS platform.

- **AWS Certified Solutions Architect – Associate**: This certification is designed for individuals with experience designing distributed applications and systems on the AWS platform. Candidates should have experience with designing and deploying scalable, highly available, and fault-tolerant systems on AWS.

- **AWS Certified SysOps Administrator – Associate**: This is a certification designed for people with experience managing and deploying applications on the AWS platform. Candidates should have experience managing and operating complex solutions on AWS.

- **AWS Certified Developer – Associate**: This certification is designed for individuals who have experience developing applications on the AWS platform. Candidates should have experience with developing and maintaining applications written for **Amazon Simple Storage Service (S3)**, **Amazon DynamoDB, Amazon Simple Queue Service (SQS), Amazon Simple Notification Service (SNS), Amazon Simple Workflow Service (SWF)**, and **AWS Elastic Beanstalk**.

- **AWS Certified Solutions Architect – Professional**: This is a certification designed for professionals who have advanced experience and knowledge of designing distributed applications and systems on the AWS platform. Candidates should be able to design solutions that run on AWS using compute, storage, networking, and security features.

- **AWS Certified DevOps Engineer – Professional**: This is a certification designed for professionals who have advanced experience and knowledge of deploying, operating, and monitoring workloads on AWS. Candidates should be able to design solutions that run on AWS using compute, storage, networking, and security features.

- **AWS Certified Security – Specialty**: This is a certification designed for professionals who have advanced experience and knowledge of securing applications and systems on the AWS platform. Candidates should be able to design solutions that run on AWS using compute, storage, networking, and security features.

- **AWS Certified Advanced Networking – Specialty**: This is a certification designed for professionals who have advanced experience and knowledge of designing and implementing complex networking solutions on the AWS platform. Candidates should be able to design solutions that run on AWS using compute, storage, networking, and security features.

- **AWS Certified Data Analytics – Specialty**: This is a certification designed for professionals who have advanced experience and knowledge of designing and implementing data analytics solutions on the AWS platform. Candidates should be able to design solutions that run on AWS using compute, storage, networking, and security features.

- **AWS Certified Machine Learning – Specialty**: This is a certification designed for professionals who have advanced experience and knowledge of designing and implementing machine learning solutions on the AWS platform. Candidates should be able to design solutions that run on AWS using compute, storage, networking, and security features.

- **AWS Certified Database – Specialty**: This is a certification designed for professionals who have advanced experience and knowledge of designing and implementing database solutions on the AWS platform. Candidates should be able to design solutions that run on AWS using compute, storage, networking, and security features.

- **AWS Certified Alexa Skill Builder – Specialty**: This certification is designed for professionals who have advanced experience in building voice-enabled Alexa skills. Candidates should be able to design solutions that run on Alexa using compute, storage, networking, and security features.

Helpful tips to become Amazon AWS certified

Like Microsoft, Amazon also provides some tips on how to approach the certification exams. This approach includes the following actions:

- **Commit to the task**: To become Amazon AWS certified, you need to commit to the task by setting aside time and resources to study and prepare for the certification exam. This includes dedicating time each day or week to study and practice using AWS services.

- **Find the proper exam for you**: Finding the proper exam that aligns with your career goals and experience level is essential for becoming AWS certified. This includes understanding the diverse types of AWS certifications available and choosing the one that best fits your career goals.

- **Develop a strategy**: Developing a strategy for studying and preparing for the certification exam is crucial for success. This includes setting goals, creating a study schedule, and identifying resources such as books, PDFs, and online training videos.

- **Use trusted resources (books, PDFs, etc.)**: Using trusted resources such as books, PDFs, and online training videos is an effective way to prepare for the certification exam. These resources can help you gain a better understanding of AWS services and how they work.

- **Practice daily**: Practicing daily by working on hands-on exercises and labs is essential for gaining practical experience with AWS services. This includes setting up test environments and experimenting with different AWS services.

- **Solve problems the AWS way**: Solving problems the AWS way is an important part of becoming AWS certified. This includes understanding how AWS services work together and how they can be used to solve real-world problems.

- **Find the right time to appear for the exam**: Finding the right time to appear for the certification exam based on your level of preparation and confidence is crucial for success. This includes taking practice exams and assessing your readiness before scheduling the actual exam.

Now that we have covered the Amazon AWS and Microsoft Azure certifications, let us now look at GCP certifications.

GCP certifications

GCP offers diverse types of certifications for distinct roles. These certifications are divided into four levels: Foundational level, Associate level, Professional level, and Additional level.

Here are some of the certification options available for Google GCP along with their descriptions:

- **Associate Cloud Engineer**: This is a certification designed for individuals who have experience working with GCP. Candidates should be able to deploy applications, monitor operations, and manage enterprise solutions.

- **Professional Cloud Architect**: This is a certification designed for professionals who have advanced experience and knowledge of designing and managing solutions on GCP. Candidates should be able to design solutions that run on GCP using compute, storage, networking, and security features.

- **Professional Data Engineer**: This is a certification designed for professionals who have advanced experience and knowledge of designing and managing data processing systems on GCP. Candidates should be able to design solutions that run on GCP using compute, storage, networking, and security features.

- **Professional Cloud Developer**: This is a certification designed for professionals who have advanced experience and knowledge of developing applications on GCP. Candidates should be able to develop applications that run on GCP using compute, storage, networking, and security features.

- **Professional Cloud Network Engineer**: This is a certification designed for professionals who have advanced experience and knowledge of designing and implementing network architectures on GCP. Candidates should be able to design solutions that run on GCP using compute, storage, networking, and security features.

- **Professional Cloud Security Engineer**: This is a certification designed for professionals who have advanced experience and knowledge of securing applications and systems on GCP. Candidates should be able to design solutions that run on GCP using compute, storage, networking, and security features.

- **Professional Collaboration Engineer**: This is a certification designed for professionals who have advanced experience in deploying and managing G Suite applications. Candidates should be able to design solutions that run on G Suite using compute, storage, networking, and security features.

- **Professional Machine Learning Engineer**: This is a certification designed for professionals who have advanced experience in designing and building machine learning models on GCP. Candidates should be able to design solutions that run on GCP using compute, storage, networking, and security features.

Helpful tips to become GCP certified

Like Microsoft and Amazon, Google also provides some tips on how to approach the certification exams. This approach includes the following actions:

- **Find training and development experience**: To become GCP certified, you need to have a foundational understanding of GCP. This includes an understanding of GCP services and how they work.

- **Develop skills specific to using GCP**: This includes learning how to design and deploy scalable, highly available, and fault-tolerant systems on GCP. You should also be familiar with the various GCP services and how they can be used to build complex systems.

- **Learning to apply GCP**: Learning how to leverage GCP for designing and processing purposes is the next step in becoming GCP certified. This includes understanding how to use GCP services such as BigQuery, Dataflow, and Dataproc for data processing and analysis.

- **Choose the right storage and database offerings**: Choosing the right storage and database offerings is crucial for building scalable and reliable systems on GCP. You should be familiar with the various storage options available on GCP, such as Cloud Storage, Cloud SQL, and Bigtable.

- **Get a grip on the enterprise case studies**: Getting a grip on enterprise case studies is an effective way to learn how to use GCP services in real-world scenarios. This includes understanding how companies are using GCP services to solve complex business problems.

- **Understand the concepts of hybrid clouds**: Understanding the concepts of the hybrid cloud is important for becoming GCP certified. This includes understanding how to integrate on-premises infrastructure with GCP services.

- **Know how to move data to Google Cloud**: Knowing how to move data to Google Cloud is essential for building scalable and reliable systems on GCP. This includes understanding how to use services such as Transfer Appliance, Transfer Service, and Storage Transfer Service.

While Microsoft, Amazon, and Google make up most of the certifications that will be achieved, there are other examples of certifications that should be mentioned.

Other certification examples

In addition to Microsoft, Amazon, and Google certification offerings, here are some alternative CSA certifications to consider:

- **CompTIA Cloud+**: This is a certification designed for professionals who have experience working in cloud computing environments. Candidates should be able to demonstrate their ability to manage and optimize cloud infrastructure services.

- **IBM Certified Solution Architect – Cloud Computing Infrastructure:** This certification is designed for professionals who have experience working with IBM Cloud. Candidates should be able to demonstrate their ability to design, plan, and architect a cloud infrastructure.

- **Oracle Cloud Infrastructure Certified Architect Associate**: This certification is designed for professionals who have experience working with Oracle Cloud Infrastructure. Candidates should be able to demonstrate their ability to design and architect solutions on Oracle Cloud Infrastructure.

At this point, the value of cloud provider certifications should be understood as helping find and land a CSA role. Also, the major cloud providers all have certification paths that enable a CSA to demonstrate skills, knowledge, and capabilities for a specific cloud provider. Also, the providers have tips on how to approach and succeed in becoming certified. Finally, there are other certifications from cloud providers and companies that might be worth looking into depending on the need for specific products or services from those companies. Now, instead of structured certification-directed learning, let us explore self-paced learning.

Self-paced learning

While traditional degrees and certifications are generally curated paths of knowledge discovery, self-paced learning can be more personal interest-oriented. All the major cloud providers offer resources to explore general topics such as architecture and design best practices, as well as more coarse-grained content such as service-specific learning modules.

Microsoft offers a free, interactive, self-paced learning platform called Microsoft Learn (`https://learn.microsoft.com/en-us/training/azure`). It provides a wide range of learning paths, modules, and labs to help you learn about Microsoft products and services, including Microsoft Azure.

AWS provides self-paced labs and AWS Skill Builder (`https://skillbuilder.aws`). Self-paced labs provide the ability to learn AWS solutions by building them in an interactive experience. Each lab focuses on a specific topic and skills to develop. Finally, Google also offers online training comprising courses, hands-on labs, and skill badges to earn via Google Cloud Training and Certification (`https://cloud.google.com/learn/training`). This training also includes targeted training for students and facility members.

Summary

This chapter was a useful guide for anyone who wants to learn more about CSA education paths and how these paths can help them advance their CSA career. It provided valuable information and insights that can help them make informed decisions and plan their learning journey.

In this chapter, background requirements were discussed for the role of CSA, such as having a technical degree or equivalent experience, as well as the pros and cons of focusing on a specific cloud computing platform provider or general cloud computing concepts.

The topic of certifications was then introduced as many CSA roles within an organization require an individual to stay current with evolving services and provide proof of competency regarding various products, services, and concepts related to cloud computing platforms.

Finally, self-paced learning was explored as a viable way to gain provider-specific training and an understanding of various provider services and concepts.

Now that we have learned about the different options to demonstrate knowledge and understanding of cloud provider platforms, let us now turn our attention to *Chapter 5, Closing In on Opportunities*. This chapter will provide options for getting experience and understanding to prepare for a formal career as a CSA.

Further reading

If you are interested in learning more about the role of CSA and the various educational options and paths available, you may want to check out the following books and online resources:

- *Cloud Solution Architect: A Complete Guide – 2021 Edition* by Gerardus Blokdyk (`https://www.amazon.com/Solutions-Architects-Handbook-Kick-start-architecture/dp/1801816611`). This book provides a complete guide to becoming a CSA. It covers topics such as CSA roles and responsibilities, CSA skills and competencies, CSA best practices and standards, CSA tools and techniques, CSA certification and training, and CSA career development. You can find this book at Barnes & Noble.

- *Cloud Academy* (`https://cloudacademy.com/`). This is an online platform that offers courses, labs, quizzes, exams, and certifications for various cloud computing platforms and topics. You can learn about cloud fundamentals, cloud security, cloud networking, cloud storage, cloud databases, cloud development, and more. You can also choose from different learning paths for different cloud computing roles such as CSA, Cloud Developer, Cloud Engineer, Cloud Administrator, and Cloud Security Specialist.

- *Coursera* (`https://www.coursera.org/browse/cloud-computing`). This is another online platform that offers courses, specializations, professional certificates, and degrees for various cloud computing platforms and topics. You can learn from leading universities and companies such as Google, AWS, Microsoft Azure, and IBM Cloud. You can also choose from different learning paths for different cloud computing roles such as CSA, Cloud Developer, Cloud Engineer, Cloud Administrator, and Cloud Security Specialist.

4

Getting Real Experience

Traditional education or specialized courses are valuable in helping you gain a fundamental understanding of concepts important to being a CSA, but they generally are not enough to fully prepare you for the role. This is because the CSA role is typically seen as a career progression from other roles that help develop the experience necessary to make good decisions as a CSA (it's often said "bad decisions lead to experience and experience leads to good decisions"). For this reason, it should be fairly rare to find CSA positions open to candidates whose background is limited to time spent in a classroom.

In this chapter, we will examine ways to increase your experience level to help you land your first work assignment as a CSA. The benefits of building out these experiences are as follows:

- Being able to develop practical skills that are not taught in traditional education
- Being able to learn how to apply theoretical knowledge to real-world problems
- Being able to stay up-to-date with the latest trends and technologies in cloud computing
- Being able to gain hands-on experience with cloud technologies
- Being able to learn from the experiences of others

While there are many ways to gain relevant experience, the following methods have been chosen for discussion because they produce the benefits discussed previously with a relatively low barrier to entry:

- Completing side projects
- Contributing to open source
- Participating and volunteering in hackathons
- Traditional internships
- Attending user groups

Completing side projects

The first way to gain real-world experience that's relevant to a CSA that we will discuss is side projects. Side projects come in two broad categories – **paid projects**, where you are doing real work for others, and **projects**, where you are working on your own doing something that resembles real work that others may need.

For the first of these categories, it's likely (and indeed recommended) that you would be working in areas that contribute to the experience you'll need as a CSA, but not performing the CSA role. On these projects, you may find yourself helping to define and implement infrastructure, writing application code, designing and implementing database schemas, helping with requirements analysis or QA testing, or several other things that contribute to the overall success of a project. The key at this point is making sure that you are looking for opportunities to contribute without putting yourself (and, by extension, your client) in the position of taking on responsibilities that you're not ready to deliver on. As you build on your experiences, it's helpful to keep in mind that many of the people considered to be the best CSAs possess what is called *T-shaped skills*. This is a term that's used to represent somebody with very broad but somewhat shallow general skills (the top of the T) and usually one area where they have developed great depth (the vertical line in the T). Pay attention to what topic areas you find to be either *take it or leave it* or a drain on you or make you feel like you're doing fulfilling work and what topic areas leave you feeling excited and energized about the work that you are doing; this will be a good guide for what you want your specific T-shaped skillset to look like. *Figure 4.1* shows an example of what the T-shaped skillset of a CSA with a security focus may look like. It's good to note that, as shown in *Figure 4.1*, there may be more than one area where someone finds themselves deeper than other areas:

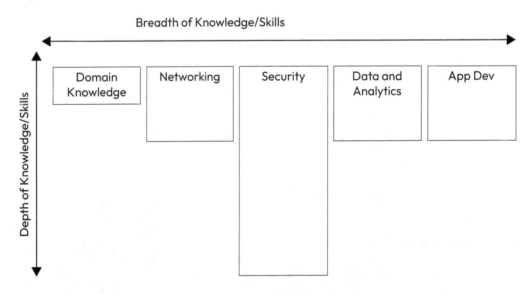

Figure 4.1 – T-shaped skillset

Paid side projects can be a little bit hard to come by, but good sources include small businesses in your network as well as dedicated websites such as Upwork (`https://www.upwork.com`), Toptal (`https://www.toptal.com`), and Field Engineer (`https://www.fieldengineer.com`). In any case, some critical aspects that are necessary to have this be a positive experience both personally and for your career growth are as follows:

- Be honest with yourself and your prospective client about where you are in your development, and don't take on more than you can handle either from a time commitment or skills perspective

- Make sure there is no room for misunderstanding regarding the services that will be provided, your schedule, and the costs involved

- Be professional – in addition to skills, you're building a reputation that will be part of what others expect from you, so make sure they expect good things!

The other type of side projects don't necessarily have a *customer* and therefore they have a pretty low barrier to entry. Because there's not a paying customer, there is also quite a bit less risk that setbacks will become part of the *permanent record* that is your professional reputation. In these projects, you can do many of the same activities as a paid project, but with two major differences:

- You are far more likely to take on tasks in the project that you wouldn't take on as an *early-in-career* member of the team, such as defining the overall architecture for the solution

- With some notable exceptions (discussed in this section), you are less likely to have other members of the project team who can give you the benefit of their experience

One source of unpaid side projects is your imagination. What kind of ideas do you have for ways that software can be used in a valuable way? Consider the following:

- In 1975, Steve Wozniak started working on a side project to design a general-purpose computing device suitable for hobbyist use. This device became the Apple I and helped start Apple Computer down the path toward becoming a household name. In May 2023, Apple announced a revenue of $94.8 billion for the second quarter of 2023 (`https://www.apple.com/newsroom/2023/05/apple-reports-second-quarter-results/`).

- Also in 1975, Paul Allen and Bill Gates started working on a side project to build a BASIC language interpreter for the Altair computer. The pair went on to create Microsoft, which has become one of the most successful computer software companies in the world. In April 2023, Microsoft reported $52.9 billion in revenue for the third quarter of fiscal year 2023 (`https://www.microsoft.com/en-us/investor/earnings/fy-2023-q3/press-release-webcast`).

What these stories (and many like them) have in common is that somebody had an idea of how they could bring something new and of value to the world and acted on it. Often, at least the initial work on these kinds of side projects can be done with a little more investment than your own time. Another common theme is that often, the most successful outcomes aren't from an individual working alone, but from the collaboration between people with complementary strengths to cover not only how to implement the idea, but also how to help other people see the value in it.

Another source of unpaid side projects is listening to or asking people around you about what you need. In 1998, I worked at the parts counter for a regional electrical supply company while studying and preparing myself for entry into my career as a professional software developer. I read everything that I could get my hands on about software design and purchased software development tools, but I lacked the imagination and *big thinking* shown by the entrepreneurs discussed previously. Instead of coming up with ideas, I asked my customers and co-workers about software that would help them. During that time, our company had just started to make price lists available for customers to download via **File Transfer Protocol (FTP)** and several of my customers said that it would save them a lot of time estimating jobs if they could integrate their pricing data in some way. I built a tool that not only integrated the pricing data that was retrieved and synchronized via FTP into their job estimates but also sent an email to us at the store when they were ready to order the materials for the job. This *side job* was largely responsible for providing the experience that I needed to formally land my first job as a software developer later that year.

Another source of *side work* that is useful for creating the opportunity to grow professionally in the experiences that you will need as a CSA is a reserve component of the military. This option may not be available everywhere and some may not be willing or able to accept the military aspect of this option, but it is worth mentioning because in the United States (where this is being written), it provides some formal education in the form of specialized schooling for the career path that you've contracted for. It also provides on-the-job training, where you can gradually increase your responsibility level for building and maintaining systems. Typically, reserve components in the United States meet for one weekend a month and members are also expected to annually complete a 2-week *advanced training* course that will either be assigned by your reserve component or selected by the reservist from among various options. Individuals who follow this path, however, should not lose sight of the fact that the reserve component does not exist simply to provide part-time jobs for people looking to gain experience – it is a military unit that has plausible potential to, at some point, become activated and members may be placed in harm's way as a result. You should not accept the benefit of this option without carefully considering your willingness to serve if called upon.

Now that you've learned how to gain experience through side projects, let's look at building experience through contributing to open source projects.

Contributing to open source

In the late 1990s, software developers looking to improve the availability and collaborative nature of software founded the open source movement. Since that time, open source software has grown in popularity. Its adoption ranges from personal usage to running some of the most critical functions of enterprise business. In 2019, Scott Hanselman blogged how an open source artificial pancreas is helping him and others live with Type 1 diabetes. Some of the benefits that are realized from using open source technology are as follows:

- Potentially lower cost (sometimes *free* can come with the hidden cost of supporting it yourself)

- For more popular packages, it can be easier to hire new team members who already understand your stack

- Code subject to public scrutiny and contribution tends to evolve in ways that are more robust, performant, and secure

- There's less worry about whether vendor insolvency will leave you unsupportable

All of this is great, but how does it help you gain the experience that you need as a CSA? It provides an open place where you can learn about the technologies that contribute to businesses where you may find employment and has a low barrier to entry. If done properly, it also provides you with the opportunity to create a progressive path, which can lead to you gaining experiences that will benefit you as a CSA and visibility that can help you land jobs in the field. In the following sections, you will learn more about that path.

Open source progression path

One of the most difficult parts of a journey is figuring out what path you want to take and why. For the journey of any early-career technologist, I recommend following a path that progressively increases direct responsibility for producing valuable improvements to the product, whether those improvements be making existing features perform better, making the existing features more reliable, or adding new features to the product. The path that's been described is not necessarily linear and is illustrated in *Figure 4.2*:

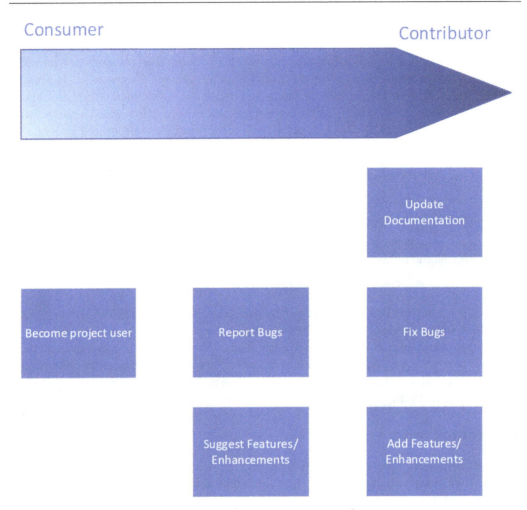

Figure 4.2 – Path from consumer to contributor

In the next section, you will start your open source progression path by becoming a user of the project.

Learn to use the product

I once heard author and speaker Dave Platt say, "Know your user – and no, you are not your user." It's critical to understand that, far too often, developers will implement features based on how they think and not how their users will intuitively use them. By starting as a user and trying to learn as much as possible about how to achieve what the software is designed to do, you can gain empathy for the end users, which will be very helpful once you get to the point where you are producing what the end users will consume.

During this stage, I also recommend becoming a reader of filed issues and change requests to gain a better feel for the project and its community. I also highly recommend looking for documentation on such things as the Code of Conduct and contribution guidelines. By convention, open source projects hosted on GitHub tend to have the following documents in the root of the repository that consumers and contributors to the project should be familiar with:

- `CODE_OF_CONDUCT.md`
- `CONTRIBUTING.md`
- `LICENSE`
- `LICENSE-CODE`
- `README.md`
- `SECURITY.md`

This is not an exhaustive list, so be sure to pay attention to the root of a given project's repository for text and markdown files.

Report bugs

All software has bugs. I tend to avoid absolutes because they are usually invalidated pretty quickly, but even in this case, where there may be some exceptions, it's important to accept that bugs are ubiquitous.

Now that we've accepted that bugs will exist, one of the best ways to get started giving back to an open source project is to make sure that those bugs are known and – just as important (if not more) – understood to the fullest extent possible.

The first step in reporting a bug is to make a succinct statement (to yourself) that would make a good headline for an article detailing the issue. One example would be *State sales tax not being added for some states*. With a clear title, contributors looking for issues in areas relevant to where they normally work can more easily find what they are going to work on next.

The next step is to write up the details of the issue in as clear and complete language as possible. At a minimum, this should include the following aspects:

- What were you trying to accomplish (and, potentially, *why*)?
- What steps led you to the unexpected behavior?
- What did you expect to happen?
- What actually happened?
- How is the issue affecting you being able to meet your goal?

If I were just a *consumer* of the open source project, I may stop at that point. Since we are talking about becoming active as a contributor to the project, I recommend going well beyond those minimum items and devising additional tests to make the nature of the behavior better understood. In the sales tax-related issue that we titled previously, this may include additional testing to understand the extent to which the problem is occurring, and the bug report would include something to the effect of *further testing showed that Alaska, Oregon, Montana, Delaware, and New Hampshire are all having this error.*

In the issue we've been describing, a developer who worked on the sales tax calculations would have sufficient information to quickly determine that the five US states being reported as missing sales tax calculations in actuality do not have state sales tax and therefore the system is correctly omitting sales tax. However, it could be that discussion of the issue may lead to a realization that simply omitting the sales tax could lead to misunderstandings and that by still showing the sales tax calculation with the state, applicable rate (0 for these states), and total tax, it will be better understood what the system is doing. In this case, even though you didn't truly discover a *bug*, you did start a conversation that led to a better experience for everyone while gaining a much deeper understanding of this project and testing.

As you grow in confidence with the project, you may find that your bug reports get much more detailed. They will likely move from watching the behavior of the system from an external point of view to understanding what is happening that is unexpected to delve into the code itself and form at least a hypothesis of where the unexpected conditions are happening in the code. Again, this may lead you to a better understanding of whether your expectations were aligned with the actual requirements, but it can also lead you to produce far more actionable information for whoever is taking action on the issue. This, in turn, may also lead to issues submitted by you to receive action sooner than ones without the level of supporting information that you are providing. Finally, adding this level of information becomes great *practice* for when you are ready to start resolving issues directly.

Update documentation

Sometimes, the *bugs* in software turn out to be incomplete or inaccurate documentation. It can be argued both ways whether incomplete documentation truly constitutes a *bug*, but inaccurate documentation falls squarely into this category. Either way, documentation updates provide a great way for you to start transitioning from *user* of the project to *contributor*.

For me, the trigger to author documentation updates for an open source project that I use usually falls into one of the following categories:

- I tried to follow the documentation to complete a task, but the documentation was inaccurate, which caused me to have to debug something

- I needed to complete a task, but I couldn't find documentation to show how, so I had to figure it out myself (possibly with help from community forums and other sources)

- The documentation is factually correct, but I found there to either be editorial issues such as spelling or grammar errors or I found existing wording to be unclear

Any time that I encounter these scenarios when trying to use open source technology, the result is that I spend more time trying to find, debug, or understand the documentation and less time working on the task that drove me to the documentation in the first place. This is the case for me and I am certain it is the case for other users of the project. A great result from going through the scenarios that I have outlined is to take notes along the way and feed those notes back to the community in the form of documentation updates that prevent them from having to go through the same discovery process that you just did.

Besides moving you along the consumer/contributor continuum, submitting pull requests with documentation updates brings some additional benefits:

- The process of making changes to the documentation makes you more familiar with the project and the feature set that is the focus of the update, and it also reinforces the experience that you gained while figuring out what needed to change

- The pull request process itself can lead to valuable interaction with other project contributors, allowing you to better understand decisions that are made in the project, be more exposed to the community, and be accepted as a contributing member

- You start to build documented experience contributing to projects, which can be helpful when demonstrating experience to potential employers

Suggest new features or enhancements to existing features

As you become more intimately familiar with the project's features, capabilities, and even its limitations and interact with other community members through things such as discussion threads on submitted issues/pull requests, blog posts, and community forums, you will likely develop some expertise in potential changes that could help the project be more useful/valuable to its served community. This is a great time to start giving back by putting the time and effort into documenting the opportunity for improvement as proposed product changes, which may be categorized as feature requests or enhancements to existing features.

When putting together proposed changes to share with the project community, it is best to start with a similar focus to what was discussed for bug reports. I find it valuable to start with a statement to capture the who, what, and why of the requirement in the form of "As [insert role here], I need [insert proposed capability here] so that [insert objective unlocked by capability]." An example of this in action could be "As a cashier, I need the system to automatically calculate sales tax so that I can collect the appropriate amount and remain compliant with laws." You may have noticed when reading the preceding sentence that the goal is stated from the end user perspective and does not include the *how* in specific implementation details. This is extremely important because technologists tend to want to make things about technology. This can often lead to the introduction of technologies for the sake of the technology instead of for how it will bring value to stakeholders.

Once you have captured the theme/objective of the proposed change, the next step is to break things down into requirements that describe the things that must be true for the objective to be met. This subject itself is worthy of dedicated books, such as Alistair Cockburn's, *Writing Effective Use Cases*. But to distill it down into points, I recommend that you think about how each requirement can be evaluated using a set of criteria referred to by the acronym **SMART**. This is important to keep in mind as you start writing enhancement proposals for open source projects:

- **Specific**: Ideally, the requirement will leave no ambiguity. For example, "the button should be easy to read" is not as specific as "the background to foreground contrast of the button should align with our accessibility standards."

- **Measurable**: There should be concrete objectives in place to know when the minimum requirement has been met. An example of this would be changing "it needs to be fast enough" to "requests should be fully processed within 2 seconds at least 90% of the time."

- **Attainable**: There is often an urge to document requirements as they would be free of constraints to balance out if implemented in a perfect world. I refer to these as *aspirational* requirements. The problem with aspirational requirements is that they establish a culture of dealing in wishes instead of things that can be committed to and acted upon. Documented requirements should take compromises into account and accurately reflect what is expected when *done*. That said, don't be so wrapped up in the *attainable* that you ignore the needs of the user. Start with a conversation about the aspirational goal and use that to iterate to a point where everyone agrees that the requirement is both attainable and effectively fulfills the need.

- **Relevant**: How does this proposed change relate to the broader goals of the project? If the requirement can't be tied back to the broader project goals, then either the requirement or the goals should be re-examined.

- **Testable**: The requirement should include enough details for the entire team to understand how to test for completion of the requirement. Often, this is left broad and open to interpretation, and when this happens, it creates an environment where bugs are more likely to be introduced and where different team members can become frustrated with each other due to mismatched interpretations.

In addition to the value that your proposed changes may bring to the project if implemented, the act of preparing, iterating over, and advocating for your change will bring you the benefit of discussion with others and having their experience contribute to you being able to think about things in a *big picture* context that considers more than just the problem that you set out to solve. It will also expose you to the compromises that are part of producing software in the real world directly. This may very well be the open source activity that most directly relates to the activities that would be part of your day-to-day as a working CSA.

Fix bugs

Now that you have been spending time becoming a subject matter expert in the project, gained familiarity with both the code and the community on the project, and used bug reports and/or feature requests as tools to solidify your understanding of how change is introduced to the project, it's time to start writing (or deleting as appropriate) some code. When looking for bugs to start contributing directly to project code, you can use the ones that you have found. In many projects, a convention has been adopted to tag some issues as *good first bugs* to help potential new contributors find a good place to start. These are usually issues that have been defined as having fairly isolated scope or are easy to understand and are less likely to have somebody working in the code base for the first time introduce wide-reaching regression bugs or become frustrated while taking on something *too big* for their experience level with the project.

Before you start working on the bug, make sure that you have followed any documentation provided in the repository or associated documentation about setting up your development environment. A developing trend on some projects is to use *dev containers* (described in the specification at `https://containers.dev`) as a way to lower the burden of having an appropriately configured development environment. Whether you have built your development environment from scratch or the project had a dev container defined to do it for you, the very first thing that I do is verify two things:

- Can I build the project from the current source code?
- Do all of the existing unit tests execute and pass?

If either or both of these answers are *no*, I am not going to introduce even the simplest change to the source code; instead, am going to have to figure out why and resolve the issue. For projects that use continuous integration to build and test whenever code is committed, you can be relatively certain that the reason you can't build and/or test on your development machine is rooted in your configuration. For projects that are not using continuous integration, solving the problem may be a much more complicated thing. Either way, if something is broken, I do not recommend making any changes that don't entirely focus on getting your build working and unit tests passing.

With a working build and passing unit tests, I am ready to start working on the bug itself. I work to reproduce the issue and prove that I am capable of making the reported issue happen at will. When I can do this, it becomes much easier to explain why it is happening and formulate code changes needed to correct the behavior. Just as I ask two questions before I start working on the project on my development machine, I ask two questions when I think I understand the nature of the bug:

- Do all of the current unit tests pass, even though the bug exists because there is a missing test?
- Do all of the current unit tests pass, even though the bug exists because there is an incorrect test?

These questions reveal that I value unit tests. This could be (and is) the topic of entire books, but I am very careful to value the pragmatic value of unit tests over dogmatic adherence to a particular methodology. I view unit tests not as a confidence measure that the software functions as expected, but as one method to increase the likelihood that changes to the code that are introduced later will be free of unintended side effects. To that end, while I appreciate high code coverage rates on any code, I want to make sure that a fixed bug has an associated unit test addition/change to guard against the bug quietly slipping back into the code.

Beyond knowing what to change and how to test the change, the other critical factor to me in working in a code base that isn't my own is to make sure that my change is congruent with the code that is already there. Within a project, it can be distracting to adjust how I read code to the style of whoever wrote a particular module or, even worse, whoever wrote a few blocks of code within a module. Instead, take it as a matter of professionalism to ensure that the only reason someone would know that you are the source of a particular change is by reviewing the history in source control.

By working on bug fixes and going through pull request processes, you can significantly increase both the breadth and depth of your experience. It's important to note, however, that this benefit does not just kick in when your pull request is approved. Whether your proposed changes are incorporated into the project or you end up with the pull request not being merged in, you still gain the benefit of the technical experience that led to your submission and the conversations with others who were part of the pull request process.

Add new features or enhancements

In many ways, adding new features or enhancements to software is easier than fixing bugs. This is because, often, you get to work from the perspective of layering something onto a product that already works as opposed to having to figure out why unexpected behaviors are happening first and then how to fix the code with the least impact on other parts of the system that are working. What does typically increase, though, is the scope of the change and the time commitment to see the change through to completion. The other major difference is that the developer will often collaborate with more team members when implementing a new feature or enhancement than fixing an acknowledged bug – before work begins on the new feature, a consensus should be built about how the new feature should work. This goes back to the SMART requirements that were discussed earlier in this chapter.

Once requirements have been agreed upon for the new feature, the process of implementing the change largely follows what we discussed for bug fixes, so we will not reiterate that here. In addition to the experiential benefits gained from fixing bugs, implementing new features can help build your reputation and provide more opportunities for you to document having produced something of value on your resume.

Now that you've learned about contributing to open source, we will look at opportunities to develop experience by participating and volunteering in hackathons.

Participating and volunteering in hackathons

A *hackathon* can have many different meanings, depending on who you ask and in what context. One common theme in the definition is that it involves a team (quite possibly an ad hoc team convened specifically for the hackathon) putting a strong focus on solving a particular problem in a short period. Many companies that value innovation will set aside time regularly where employees are encouraged to shift focus from their day-to-day duties and participate in a hackathon. The companies anticipate that some of the innovations coming out of the exercise will become improvements to the company's products or services.

During a hackathon, you will typically be exposed to an entire iteration of the software life cycle in as few as a couple of days. This can include establishing what value you're going to deliver, assigning roles that team members will play based on what they are already good at or (better yet) where they would like to gain additional experience, defining requirements, and building and testing the solution. It can have the effect of building a month's worth of experiences in a matter of days.

That's great to broaden and/or deepen your T-shaped skills if you already work for a company that has incorporated hackathons, but this chapter is supposed to be about gaining the experience needed to help you get that job! In the following sub-sections, I am going to discuss two different kinds of hackathon opportunities that can be done outside of a work context.

Volunteer events

Some organizations, such as GiveCamp (`https://givecamp.org`), connect charitable organizations with needs such as implementing a cloud-based system for volunteers with the willingness and skills to help meet those needs. To maximize the potential availability of volunteers largely drawn from the professional community, these events are often held over a weekend. Specific GiveCamp events that I have attended had participants meet up on Friday evening for kick-off and conduct presentations of the final product on Sunday afternoon. I found it to be an intense and exhausting event, but it was valuable in the new experiences that it provided me and I felt good about providing value to organizations that would, in turn, go on to help others.

Hack-themed learning events

Technology companies are continuing to realize the value of experiential learning over what learners have grown to expect from a *class*. In response, many are adopting learning events where the role of *instructor* transitions to *facilitator* or *coach*, and the majority of the learning that comes from the event is the students teaching each other. In cases where a member of the team has relevant experience to share with the rest of the team, that member shares knowledge. In cases where nobody has relevant experience, the team navigates research and experimentation to come to a workable solution.

Cloud providers Microsoft and **Amazon Web Services** (**AWS**) both have experiential learning programs that are designed to help accelerate people learning their platforms and cloud computing in general – AWS has GameDay and Microsoft has OpenHack or What the Hack.

AWS GameDay (`https://aws.amazon.com/gameday/`) is a gamified learning program where teams compete for bragging rights by implementing solutions to realistic business problems using AWS services. This experience is free of charge, but in many cases, it's only open to employers who are Amazon partners.

Microsoft has a formal program called OpenHack Microsoft has a formal program called OpenHack in which participants in which participants become part of a team focused on solving problems related to a specific technology or discipline. Topics include things such as DevOps, AI-powered knowledge mining, serverless, and containers, among others. During this program, Microsoft coaches help make sure that an effective learning environment exists while team members work through challenges. These events have always been free of charge and were traditionally held in person until the COVID-19 pandemic caused them to start being delivered virtually. You can check the OpenHack website for current topics and schedules.

With the popularity of the formal OpenHack program, Microsoft employees wanted to bring their users a much broader set of topics that could be consumed *on demand* and delivered by Microsoft, their partners, or even end users who have become subject matter experts and could be contributed to by the community as a whole. This idea became *What The Hack* (`https://github.com/ microsoft/WhatTheHack`), which is a collection of challenge-based hack-a-thons that include a student guide, coach guide, lecture presentations, sample/instructional code, and templates to allow anyone to conduct an event, similar to what is offered by OpenHack. What The Hack provides a structure in which you and your local community (such as a cloud computing user group) can build learning opportunities around to increase your experience.

The one caveat that I will provide regarding gamified challenge-based learning experiences is that any time gamification comes into the mix, there's a natural human drive to *game the system*. One way that I've seen this done is that people will work through content on their own before attending an event and show up ready to impress everyone with how quickly they complete the challenges. Don't be that attendee – it not only erodes the benefit that you will receive by working through the challenges as part of a team but it also potentially ruins the experience for the other members of your team, who will now spend their time watching you blaze a trail through the challenges instead of being able to learn by working through them.

Now that you have learned about short-term volunteering and hackathons as ways to increase your experience level, let's take a look at more traditional internship opportunities.

Traditional internships

This chapter has covered some less traditional ways that someone new to a career in CSA can accelerate gaining experience, but for those for whom it is available, the value of a traditional internship should not be ignored. In a typical internship experience, students spend time working with an employer to apply what they are learning in the classroom to the real world. In addition to reinforcing what is being learned in the classroom, interns also gain the benefit of being exposed to a work setting, which can be very different than that of a university.

Some of the benefits that are gained by participating in an internship program are as follows:

- Many internships offer the opportunity to earn while learning
- Interns get the opportunity to demonstrate what value they could bring to an employer without dealing with the stigma of being inexperienced
- Internship experience may ease a student's transition to *office life*

- Over several years, interns may sample different employers and learn more about what they do or don't want in an employer after graduation

- Often, interns are given the opportunity to transition to a full-time employment status following graduation

If you are currently in school, a great place to start learning about internship opportunities is your guidance counselor. Some employers also directly accept applications for internships, so if there are companies that are high on your list of desirable employers, you should check the careers section of their website for internship opportunities.

While not technically an internship, many technology companies have formalized programs for hiring and developing recent college graduates who show promise. These programs often involve a rotation through various job functions, which helps the early in-career employees discover where they can flourish (the *deep* part of their T-shaped skills) and also gives a well-rounded view of the organization as a whole (the *broad* part of their T-shaped skills). Even if you've already graduated, be sure to look for recent graduate programs at prospective employers.

Now that you have learned about traditional internships, let's finish this section by discussing how attending user groups can help you build experience.

Attending user groups

The final way you can build on your formal education is to become involved in one or more local user group communities focused on technology and cloud computing. You will likely start as a *listener* in the community, hearing about challenges that other attendees are facing, how they have tried to solve them, and advice being given to them by others with relevant experience. The goal should be to transition to become an active participant in the discussion as you continue to learn more and at least understand the context. You don't have to necessarily give advice to participate in these discussions, but you can ask questions that will both help solidify your understanding and potentially cause others to look at things from an angle that's not been considered before.

Besides the open discussions often found in user groups, often, these groups have presentations on specific topic areas at their regular meetings. These may be presented by guest speakers who are joining as resident experts, but just as often, they are given by members of the user groups themselves. As with participation in the open discussions, you don't necessarily have to be considered an expert to share things that you are working on and learning with other group members. Preparing and delivering a presentation may help you develop skills in the following ways:

- It can help improve communication skills and overcome timidity as you can present to groups and answer questions that stem from your presentation.

- It can help you learn how to structure information to be presented in an organized and concise format. This will make you better able to communicate ideas at work.

- Doing research and testing to prepare presentations and any related demos can further deepen your knowledge of the topic area.

Finally, another advantage of becoming involved in local user groups is that employers and recruiters often attend these groups looking for people to hire. They may hear questions you're asking or see your presentations and see you as someone who has the potential to bring great value to their company. Investing in your professional growth by committing time to these groups is often seen as a sign that you will be a committed and professional employee.

Summary

In this chapter, we discussed how traditional education by itself is not well suited to fully prepare someone to be a CSA and how the CSA role typically requires a blend of skills and knowledge that is gained by experience in several related roles. We also discussed several ways that somebody can accelerate the development of their CSA-related skills. This included completing side projects, contributing to open source, participating and volunteering in hackathons and traditional internships, and attending user groups.

As a parting thought from this chapter, I would encourage you to not think of experience as being a construct related to time itself, but instead related to what you have seen and done within that time. It is easy to get caught in the "Sam has been working in the career field for 10 years, so they must be an expert" frame of thought without considering whether the individual (including yourself) truly has 10 years of experience or has repeated the same year's worth of experience 10 times. Be constantly looking for ways to experience new things that will broaden and/or deepen your T-shaped skillset.

In the past couple of chapters, you have learned about building knowledge, skills, and experience to help you prepare yourself for CSA opportunities. In the next chapter, you will learn how to identify the right CSA opportunities for you.

5

Closing In on Opportunities

Your personality type and personal interests can help determine what industry, organization, and type of role you should pursue. In many cases, **Cloud Solution Architects (CSAs)** follow personal areas of interest such as automotive, healthcare, or financial services, which keeps their role interesting and makes it easier to stay current with new and emerging trends. The journey of landing a CSA role starts with the general industry of interest. Next, decide on start-up or well-established companies. Finally, decide which business unit is the most desirable – IT or business-aligned groups. If the decision is too difficult, consulting or contract work might help you explore before committing. By the end of this chapter, you should be ready to look for specific job offerings based on outcomes from this part of the journey as described in the sections of this chapter.

To achieve readiness, this chapter will cover the following topics aligned with the journey:

- Finding an industry that suits you
- Small start-up versus large enterprise
- Working in an IT organization versus a business unit
- Research resources: Finding the opportunities

Let us begin this journey by understanding the differences in the CSA role across various industries and how that might affect a CSA role.

Finding an industry that suits you

CSAs find employment across nearly every industry, from technology and manufacturing firms to game developers, digital design companies, and healthcare providers. Major software and hardware technology companies such as Amazon, Microsoft, and Google demand the expertise of CSAs to design, manage, and enhance their cloud infrastructure. Moreover, as cloud computing gains prominence beyond the tech sector, non-technically oriented companies actively recruit CSAs in increasing numbers.

According to the U.S. Bureau of Labor Statistics (`https://www.bls.gov/iag/`), as of 2023, industries in the United States can be categorized into two super sector groups: goods-producing industries and service-providing industries. Combined, these two super sectors are comprised of 10 sectors and each sector will have common trends relating to the pace of technology adoption, such as moving to cloud computing. Let us take a closer look at each sector, also known as industry, and what types of technologies are leveraged in each.

Construction

This industry is involved in the construction of buildings and other structures. Also, architecture and design, as well as engineering, are roles within the construction industry. Typical hardware and software technology used in the construction industry include the following:

- **Building Information Modelling (BIM):** This is a digital representation of the physical and functional characteristics of a facility. BIM involves creating an interactive 3D model with direct collaboration from architects, engineers, contractors, and other construction domain experts.

- **3D printing:** This is used to create building components.

- **Drones:** These are used for surveying, mapping, and inspection.

- **Robotics:** These are used for tasks such as bricklaying and welding.

- **Automated equipment:** This includes excavators and bulldozers.

The common theme in the preceding technologies list is the fact that each of these capabilities typically requires a data center/cloud type of implementation to support the data ingestion, processing, and storage. Also, while these technologies are leveraged in the construction industry, they are likely going to be produced as a product by a hardware or software provider.

Managing substantial amounts of data from various sources such as BIM (mentioned previously) and **geographic information systems (GIS)** is also common in construction technologies. Additionally, the construction industry often involves working with multiple stakeholders such as architects, engineers, contractors, and subcontractors. As a result, integrating different systems and applications can be a challenge. The CSA role becomes extremely important in this regard to ensure all requirements are met and the products and services recommended can support the stakeholders' needs. Next, let us understand the education and health services industry.

Education and health services

The education and health services industry is involved in providing education and health services to people both in-person as well as remotely via a video conferencing type of technology. Typical hardware and software technology used in the education and health services industry include the following:

- **Telehealth or telemedicine:** This is the enablement of devices, networks, and video communication software to deliver healthcare services from a distance.

- **Digital health and telehealth technologies**: These are used by students and professionals to receive training in their area of the field and to treat patients remotely.

- **Learning Management Systems (LMSs)**: These are used for online learning.

- **Video games**: These are used for educational purposes.

- **Voice search**: This is used for searching for medical information.

The education and health services industry deals with sensitive data such as personal health information and student records. As a result, data security and privacy are critical concerns.

Also, like the construction industry, the education and health services industry often involves managing enormous amounts of data from various sources such as electronic health records and student information systems.

In this industry, security is very important to provide protection from personal health information regarding health histories and patient records. The role of the CSA tends to focus not only on using the right products and services in a solution architecture but also on making sure they are secure and compliant with various regulatory concerns that cover the education and health services industry.

Another industry with high-security needs and regulatory compliance is the financial activities industry. We can now explore that industry and the objectives of the CSA role.

Financial activities

This industry is involved in providing financial services such as banking, insurance, and investment management. Typical hardware and software technology used in the financial activities industry include the following:

- **Mobile banking**: This enables customers to use their mobile devices to access accounts and perform transactions with their bank. Online banking allows customers to perform transactions and access their bank accounts using the internet from any supported device with an internet connection, usually via a web browser.

- **Digital wallets**: These allow customers to store their credit card information on their mobile devices and make payments using their mobile devices.

- **Cryptocurrencies**: These are a form of digital money that uses cryptography to control how new coins are created and how transactions are verified.

- **Artificial intelligence (AI)**: This is used for fraud detection and prevention.

The financial activities industry involves managing copious amounts of data from various sources such as customer transactions and financial records.

Additionally, the financial activities industry often involves working with multiple stakeholders such as banks, insurance companies, and investment firms. As a result, integrating different systems and applications can be a challenge. An example of a solution architecture that demonstrates a decentralized trust can be seen in *Figure 5.1*:

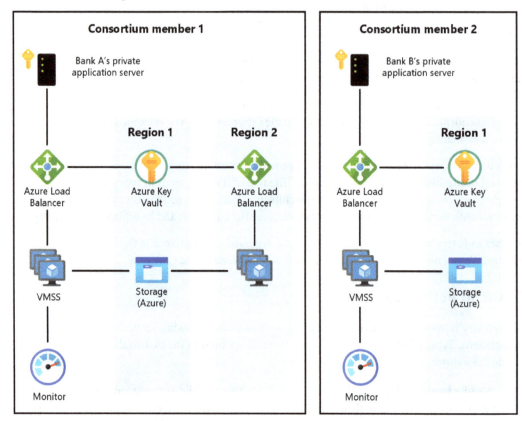

Figure 5.1 – Decentralized trust example architecture

The preceding diagram represents a very simple distributed ledger network between two banks. Bank A and Bank B can read each other's nodes for banking transactions to confirm that a transaction took place.

Because this industry is heavily regulated, the adoption of innovative technology takes time. This is because the products or services need to be proven secure and reliable. Given this pace of adoption, a CSA in the financial activities industry could spend a good amount of time working on systems that are older and less innovative. In some cases, though, the opposite is true. In the cryptocurrency business, solutions that include blockchain (distributed ledger system) and containers (lightweight virtualization of servers) are very common.

Next, we will pivot to an industry that works with much larger volumes of data and content: the information industry.

Information

This industry is involved in the creation, processing, and distribution of information and content. This can include everything from newspapers to online blogs to domain-specific content, such as healthcare or legal content. Generally, not only is the information made available to large groups of people, but it is usually searchable for easy access to topics of interest by an individual. Typical hardware and software technology used in the information industry include the following:

- Search engines, such as Google, allow users to search for information on the internet

- Social media platforms, such as Facebook, allow users to connect with each other and share information

- **Big data analytics**: This is used to analyze substantial amounts of data to identify patterns and trends

- **AI**: This is used for natural language processing and image recognition

Because the content and information are usually categorized and searchable, a significant amount of work is spent optimizing the storage solutions and making sure they are secure and highly performant. Analytics are applied to the content, in many cases to see what patterns exist, but also to determine if there is any value in the content to monetize it. Also, to include the content of an image or video/audio recording, AI is usually involved in doing speech-to-text conversions and object recognition in images and videos.

In the information industry, a CSA can spend a significant amount of time tweaking existing service deployments in the cloud to make sure storage is performance and cost-optimized. Bad design decisions can lead to higher latency and costly capabilities. Generally, when a CSA designs solution architectures for this industry, they tend to make sure compute-based resources are provisioned closely to their storage services for performance reasons. This also helps control costs when data is not constantly being ingested and egressed to/from the cloud platform.

While the information industry is largely producing a product of information, the next industry is focused on providing services. Let us now look at the leisure and hospitality industry.

Leisure and hospitality

This industry is involved in providing leisure and hospitality services such as hotels, restaurants, and entertainment. All these services are backed by systems that keep track of their relationship with the customer so they can provide tailored and individual experiences in many situations. In addition to **customer relationship management** (**CRM**) systems, typical hardware and software technology used in the leisure and hospitality industry include the following:

- **Mobile apps**: These allow customers to book reservations and order food and drink

- **Social media platforms**: These are used to promote events and connect with customers

- **AI**: This is used for personalized recommendations and customer service

Cross-selling and up-selling are revenue generators in this industry, so AI is applied in situations where additional product recommendations can be presented to the customer. AI can also be leveraged when the business is trying to convince the customer to purchase an upgrade, such as better seats at a concert or a bigger hotel room. In entertainment, it is very common for special effects to be a part of the show. These effects are often driven by systems that run on cloud computing platforms. For a CSA role, there is a broad range of opportunities from traditional back-office IT systems, to advanced special effects configuration and control systems that focus on **Internet of Things (IoT)** solutions, such as camera, drone, and light controllers.

Another industry that deals with IoT as a core technology is manufacturing. Let us focus on exploring the manufacturing industry now.

Manufacturing

This industry is involved in the production of goods using raw materials or components. Often, assembly lines in a manufacturing facility include robots or other devices that are configured to operate without much human intervention. Because these devices require ongoing maintenance and observability to ensure smooth operation, the following hardware and software technologies are used in the manufacturing industry:

- **Robotics**: These are used for tasks such as welding, painting, and assembly
- **3D printing**: This is used to create prototypes and parts
- **IoT**: This is used to monitor and optimize production processes
- **Augmented reality (AR)**: This is used for training and maintenance

For a CSA, a considerable amount of time will revolve around IoT device provisioning, telemetry processing, operational support, and historical data processing. This is in addition to traditional back-office IT types of tasks such as operating system updates and security monitoring. Given manufacturing facilities can often be in regions where connectivity to the internet is unreliable, a CSA must include solution architectures that support scenarios where the facility can continue to operate with access to cloud computing platforms. An example of this architecture can be seen in *Figure 5.2*:

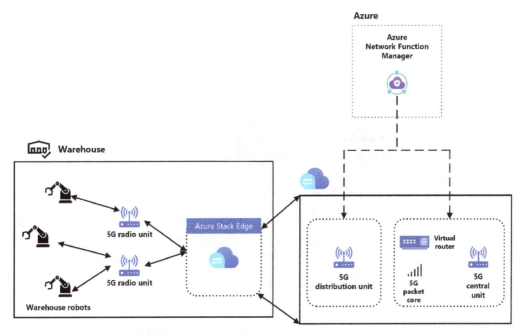

Figure 5.2 – Assembly plant architecture example

The preceding diagram represents an assembly plant solution architecture that entails a hybrid approach where an edge appliance is provisioned to control devices on the assembly plant floor, which includes the 5G wireless protocol standard for low-latency networking.

Before manufacturing can occur, the materials often used to create products need to be collected and refined for use. Let us now explore the natural resources and mining industry, which is critical to manufacturing products.

Natural resources and mining

This industry is involved in the extraction of natural resources such as oil, gas, and minerals. Like the manufacturing industry, IoT technologies play a pivotal role in effectively and efficiently mining natural resources. Common solutions adopted in the natural resources and mining industry include the following:

- **Drones**: These are used for surveying and mapping

- **Autonomous vehicles**: These are used for transportation and hauling

- **IoT**: This is used to monitor and optimize production processes

- **AI**: This is used for predictive maintenance and quality control

- **AR**: This is used for training and maintenance

Monitoring and managing heavy equipment used to mine resources generally require IoT technologies. Because of this, CSA skills tend to transfer between manufacturing and the natural resources and mining industries.

A current trend in this industry involves pivoting towards replacing finite resources with renewal resources. A well-known example is shifting from coal-based fuels to solar and wind energy. As these technologies become more common, a CSA is likely to design or implement management systems for solar grids or wind farms. Also, AI/**machine learning** (**ML**) (described in *Chapter 4*, *Getting Real Experience*) is common regarding predictive analytics and weather trends and sun exposure for a given region.

Professional and business services

This industry includes a wide range of services such as legal services, accounting services, and consulting services. Given the broad range of work that happens in this industry, there are several different technologies that are common, including the following:

- **Cloud computing**: This allows businesses to store and access data over the internet
- **AI**: This is used for predictive analytics and customer service
- **CRM software**: This is used to manage customer interactions and data

In this industry, it is very common for time-tracking solutions for people to provide invoices for billable time. Another common solution is resource management to avoid having employees sitting idle and not billing customers.

For a CSA, these products are more likely to be implemented or extended on cloud platforms as opposed to building custom solution architectures. It is also very likely that these products are presented as **Software-as-a-Service** (**SaaS**) solutions, which limits the amount of customization to the product.

While the professional and business services industry generally involves people providing a service, the next industry focuses more on vehicles and infrastructure as the primary mechanism to provide services or resources. Let us now pivot toward the trade, transportation, and utilities industry.

Trade, transportation, and utilities

This industry includes businesses involved in the transportation of goods and people, the sale of goods at retail or wholesale, and the provision of utility services such as electricity and water. Common technology used in the trade, transportation, and utilities industry includes the following:

- **Autonomous vehicles**: These are used for transportation and hauling
- **IoT**: This is used to monitor and optimize production processes
- **AI**: This is used for predictive maintenance and quality control

This industry is currently evolving at a rapid pace as automotive and fleet vehicle companies are evolving toward more autonomous driving capabilities. For CSAs, AI/ML systems are at the forefront of these capabilities and require significant compute resources to provide relay simulations and data model training. A simple example of this solution architecture can be seen in *Figure 5.3*:

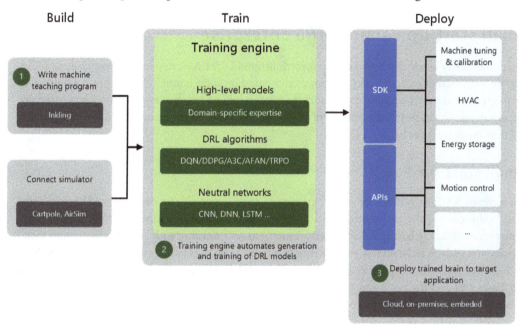

Figure 5.3 – AI/ML autonomous systems sample architecture

Also, in the vehicles, there is a considerable amount of hardware to provide telemetry to the onboard compute resources to make decisions on speed, direction, and collision avoidance. These devices require an IoT platform for monitoring and management.

In the preceding sample architecture, the workflow logically moves from step one (data collection) to step two (using the data to train the algorithm) to step three (deploying the algorithm to the vehicle).

While all the industries discussed until this point have clear definitions and technologies associated with them, the next industry is relatively vague and broad. We will now turn our attention to the other services industry.

Other services (except public administration)

This industry includes a wide range of services such as repair and maintenance, personal care services, and religious organizations. Given the industry topic is so broad, it is hard to define specific technologies or solution architectures a CSA will be required to create and support. Somewhat common across this industry is the need for Human Resources systems, payroll and billing/timekeeping, and other IT back-office systems. For a CSA, solution architectures would look very similar to on-premises solutions, especially if the services used in the architecture are based on the Infrastructure as a Service model. Now that industries have been explored, the next criteria to consider is the size of the organization and what considerations should be taken.

Small start-up versus large enterprise

Once an industry is selected based on the preceding options, the next step in securing a role as a CSA is to decide whether to filter potential companies based on their maturity. One option would be to try to get a job at a start-up company. Another option would be to target a well-established company. Depending on the industry, the options of one versus the other might be limited, but it is important to know the differences between the two.

Small start-up

It is common for CSAs working for a start-up company to be responsible for designing and implementing cloud solutions for the entire organization. The evaluation and selection of cloud providers are common, establishing best practices for cloud adoption, and working with IT teams to monitor cloud privacy and address technical issues is likely going to be a part of the CSA role. Other responsibilities include meeting with company executives to understand the organization's goals, maintaining cloud databases and existing programs and architecture, and training other members of the IT team on various cloud-computing technologies.

In addition to technical skills, basic business skills such as calculating return on investment, reading financial statements, and the basics of what C-level executives care about are prerequisites.

Working for a start-up company can be exciting and challenging. Working on innovative technologies and being part of a team that is potentially disrupting any of the industries mentioned previously is very possible. However, working for a start-up can also be stressful and demanding. A CSA will likely work long hours and take on multiple roles within the company. The CSA may also be asked to do so with a more limited budget and fewer resources. It is also very common in a start-up to work on many projects and design multiple solution architectures in parallel. This can be very different from working in a mature, large enterprise, which we will now discuss.

Large enterprise

A CSA working for a large enterprise will commonly be responsible for designing, developing, implementing, and supporting cloud-computing solutions, but usually for a business unit or a smaller section of the company's cloud-computing solutions. In addition to providing software and products as a service to customers, a CSA may also be responsible for ensuring all the applications used in-house, by customers or suppliers integrate, which can take a considerable amount of time and effort. CSAs will also be responsible for moving non-cloud systems into the cloud, securing the cloud, and assessing the risk of working with third-party cloud providers and platforms.

Working for a well-established large enterprise, a CSA can expect to have more people to collaborate with. Some of those people can be more experienced colleagues who can mentor a CSA in their career path decisions and strategic direction.

As a CSA, you will provide recommendations and roadmaps for proposed solutions, perform design, debug, and performance analysis on solutions, document and share best practice knowledge for innovative solutions, advocate for process improvements and help develop solutions, and regularly communicate new features and benefits to partners, customers, and other stakeholders.

Small start-ups will either fail or grow over time. If the company grows, the role of the CSA may change over time as the small start-up becomes a large enterprise. It may also be acquired by another company and become a part of a larger enterprise business. Either way, the next decision is whether to look for a role in an IT organization or try to find a job aligned with a business unit. Let us now explore the difference between IT and business units and what to expect working in each.

Working in an IT organization versus a business unit

A CSA working in an IT organization is responsible for designing and implementing cloud-based solutions that meet the organization's needs. They work closely with other IT professionals to ensure that the solutions are scalable, secure, and reliable. On the other hand, a CSA working in a business unit is responsible for designing and implementing cloud-based solutions that meet the specific needs of the business unit. They work closely with business stakeholders to ensure that the solutions are aligned with the business goals.

Next, a CSA working in an IT organization has a broader focus on the entire organization's IT infrastructure. They need to ensure that the cloud-based solutions they design and implement integrate seamlessly with other IT systems and processes. A CSA working in a business unit has a narrower focus on the specific business unit's needs. They need to ensure that the cloud-based solutions they design and implement meet the specific requirements of the business unit.

Also, a CSA working in an IT organization needs to have a broad range of technical skills related to cloud computing, such as cloud architecture, security, networking, and storage, or be very focused on one of the technology domains discussed in *Chapter 2, Types of Cloud Solution Architect Roles*. They also need to have excellent communication skills to work effectively with other IT professionals across the organization. A CSA working in a business unit needs to have excellent communication skills to work effectively with business stakeholders. They also need to have strong problem-solving skills to understand and address the specific challenges faced by the business unit.

Another difference is culture. The culture of an IT organization is often more focused on technology and innovation than on business goals. In contrast, the culture of a business unit is often more focused on achieving specific business goals than on technology and innovation.

Finally, a career path needs to be considered. A CSA working in an IT organization may have more opportunities for career advancement within the IT department or across different departments within the organization. In contrast, a CSA working in a business unit may have fewer opportunities for career advancement outside of their current role.

Now that we have considered industries, maturity levels of companies, and departments, let us turn our focus to finding opportunities based on the criteria for each of these topics.

Research resources – finding the opportunities

Now that the industry has been selected, the preferred company size has been determined, and whether to work in IT or a business unit has been answered, the next step is to start looking for job opportunities. Some opportunities present themselves in obvious places such as company websites or online job boards. Others may be presented via various friends or networking connections. Let us explore these resources in more depth.

Career section of company websites

Many companies have a section of their website dedicated to careers/jobs available. If a specific company desires a CSA, this might be the best place to start looking for a job opportunity. If a specific company is not part of the job selection criteria, other resources can help narrow down the job search.

Conferences

Conferences can provide a terrific opportunity to network with CSAs and technologists working for various companies. These people will tend to be open and honest about the pros and cons of their employer. Sometimes, these people are a better source of the reality of the employer versus a job posting or a recruiter. The following conferences have a high potential for networking:

- **AWS re:Invent** (https://reinvent.awsevents.com/): AWS re:Invent is a learning conference hosted by AWS for the global cloud computing community. The in-person event features keynote announcements, training and certification opportunities, access to 2,000+ technical sessions, the Expo, after-hours events, and so much more.

- **Google Cloud Next** (https://cloud.withgoogle.com/next): Google Cloud Next is an annual conference hosted by Google Cloud for developers and IT professionals who want to learn about the latest cloud technologies from Google Cloud experts.

- **Microsoft Build** (https://build.microsoft.com/): Microsoft Build is an annual conference hosted by Microsoft for developers who want to learn about the latest technologies from Microsoft experts.

Sometimes, attending a conference can be cost-prohibitive, especially if flights and hotels are a part of the costs. If this is the case, professional networking sites and online job boards can be very useful in finding a CSA role. Also, explore the opportunity to get involved in local user groups related to cloud computing. Many user groups can be found on the website `https://www.meetup.com`.

Networking and online job boards

Networking and online job boards usually have a free version and a premium paid version. Generally, when looking for a CSA role, the free version should be adequate to start the job search process. While the following list is not exhaustive, it does represent some of the more visited, commonly used sites for a job search and a brief description of what type of functionality it provides:

- **LinkedIn** (`https://www.linkedin.com/`): LinkedIn is a great resource for networking and connecting with other professionals in the industry. It also has a job search feature where users can search for jobs and apply directly through the site. Many companies also post job listings on LinkedIn.

- **Indeed** (`https://www.indeed.com/`): Indeed is a great resource for job listings as it aggregates job listings from various sources such as company career pages, job boards, and staffing agencies. It also has a resume builder feature where users can create a resume and apply for jobs directly through the site.

- **Glassdoor** (`https://www.glassdoor.com/`): Glassdoor provides company reviews, salary reports, and interview questions from current and former employees. This information can be useful when researching companies and preparing for interviews. It also has a job search feature where users can search for jobs and apply directly through the site.

- **Monster** (`https://www.monster.com/`): Monster is a great resource for job listings as it aggregates job listings from various sources such as company career pages, job boards, and staffing agencies. It also has a resume builder feature where users can create a resume and apply for jobs directly through the site.

- **Dice** (`https://www.dice.com/`): Dice specializes in technology jobs and aggregates job listings from various sources such as company career pages, job boards, and staffing agencies. This makes it a great resource for finding technology jobs such as CSAs.

Summary

This chapter has helped an aspiring CSA close in on opportunities to take a role within an organization. First, 10 industries were explored. Each industry has a specific area of expertise to develop and has opportunities for a CSA to play a critical role in a company's success within each industry. Also, each industry has unique attributes that determine the potential type of work a CSA will do as part of day-to-day activities.

Next, small start-ups and large enterprises were compared to see what type of differences a CSA would encounter when working for each type of company. Both have pros and cons, and neither is perfect.

Thirdly, as part of the process of landing a CSA role, a comparison between IT organizations and business units was explored to see what type of work environment is provided and how collaboration happens.

Lastly, research resources were addressed so that when the topics previously mentioned were addressed and considered, landing the role of a CSA becomes less difficult to filter through all of the potential opportunities that may exist.

In the next chapter, we will move on to exploring what preparation is necessary to pursue a role as a CSA and what techniques can be used to stand out from other candidates.

Part 3: Prepare for and After the Offer

Your job hunt for a cloud solution architect role has been successful – now what? We explore the next step in the journey and how to stay successful as a cloud solution architect.

This part has the following chapters:

6
Time to Pursue the Job

In *Chapter 5, Closing In on Opportunities*, we filtered our job criteria based on the industry, the maturity of the company, and the size of the organization. Now that the pursuit of the role has started, there are still a few factors to consider that affect the chances of landing a **cloud solutions architect** (**CSA**) role, such as level of experience and responsibility, compensation expectations, resume quality, and social media presence.

As we have explored in previous chapters, not all CSA roles are the same. Depending on the level of experience and responsibility, a CSA can be classified as junior, senior, or principal. Each level has distinct roles and expectations, as well as different salary ranges and career paths.

Another crucial factor worth considering is the market demand and supply for CSAs. The job market for CSAs is dynamic and competitive, and it varies by region, industry, domain, and organization. Understanding the market trends and conditions for CSAs in a specific target area and sector when negotiating a realistic compensation package is critical.

The most crucial tool needed for a CSA job search is the resume. An outstanding resume is a document that shows skills, experience, and achievements in cloud computing to potential employers, hiring managers, and recruiters. Highlighting results and outcomes that demonstrate impact and value as a CSA is critical to getting the interview with the prospective employer.

Another important self-marketing tool is social media. It is especially important to update social media sites to reflect status, goals, and qualifications as a CSA. Social media sites are powerful tools for building a personal brand, highlighting work and skills, and connecting with potential employers and recruiters.

Given the importance of the aforementioned topics, we will go into more detail in the following sections:Deciding to pursue a junior, senior, or principal CSA role?

- Understanding the market and your worth
- Making your resume stand out

- Updating social media sites
- Preparing interview questions

Let us get started preparing to pursue the job by assessing the different common levels of experience for a CSA and which one makes sense to target.

Deciding to pursue a junior, senior, or principal CSA role?

When deciding to enter the job market targeting a CSA role, it is important to decide what level of experience aligns with the work experience you have. Typically, there are three general levels of CSA: junior, senior, and principal. Different organizations may have slightly different names and requirements for these levels, but they will look very similar to the three mentioned. Let us explore each level in more detail.

Junior CSA

A junior CSA is an entry-level position that may require a bachelor's degree in computer science, engineering, or a related field, as well as some relevant certifications such as AWS Certified Solutions Architect - Associate or Microsoft Certified: Azure Solutions Architect Expert. Related job experience may also be considered in lieu of a degree or certifications. A junior CSA typically has less than three years of experience in cloud computing and learns from senior or principal CSAs while working on smaller or less complex projects. Designing and implementing basic cloud solutions, such as migrating applications to the cloud, setting up cloud environments, and troubleshooting issues, are some of the responsibilities of a junior CSA. A junior CSA must also have good communication skills and be able to collaborate with other team members and stakeholders.

A good candidate for the junior CSA level has a solid foundation in cloud computing concepts and technologies, but might still need guidance and supervision from more experienced CSAs. This candidate is eager to learn new skills and improve existing ones, and is willing to take on challenges and responsibilities within their scope of knowledge. Finally, the ideal candidate can work well with others and communicate effectively with technical as well as non-technical audiences.

If you believe that you have more experience or qualifications than what is mentioned here, let us explore the senior CSA level for consideration.

Senior CSA

A senior CSA is a mid-level position that may require a bachelor's or master's degree in computer science, engineering, or a related field, as well as several relevant certifications, such as AWS Certified Solutions Architect – Professional or Microsoft Certified: Azure DevOps Engineer Expert. A senior CSA typically has more than three years of experience in cloud computing and leads or manages medium-to-large-scale projects. Designing and implementing complex cloud solutions, such as developing cloud-native applications, integrating multiple cloud services, and optimizing cloud performance and security, are some of the responsibilities of a senior CSA. A senior CSA must also have excellent communication skills and be able to mentor junior CSAs, as well as present and explain cloud architectures to senior management and clients.

A senior CSA will have a deep understanding of cloud computing concepts and technologies and can apply them to various scenarios and domains. This candidate is confident in their personal abilities and skills, and can lead or manage projects independently or with minimal supervision. This level may require the ability to mentor junior CSAs and to demonstrate expertise and value to senior management and clients.

The senior CSA role is a great fit for most candidates.

If your education, experience, and understanding of cloud computing solutions architecture are beyond the senior level, the next role of principal CSA is worth considering.

Principal CSA

A principal CSA is a senior-level position that may require a doctoral degree in computer science, engineering, or a related field, as well as multiple relevant certifications, such as AWS Certified Solutions Architect – Specialty or Microsoft Certified: Azure Solutions Architect Expert. A principal CSA typically has more than seven years of experience in cloud computing and oversees or directs large-scale or strategic projects. Designing and implementing innovative cloud solutions, such as creating new cloud products or services, solving challenging cloud problems, and advancing cloud best practices, are some of the responsibilities of a principal CSA. A principal CSA must also have outstanding communication skills and be able to influence and inspire junior and senior CSAs, as well as establish and maintain relationships with key stakeholders and partners.

A typical candidate for the principal CSA level has a comprehensive knowledge of cloud computing concepts and technologies and can create novel solutions that address complex or emerging needs. This person is already an authority in the cloud computing field and a visionary leader who can drive innovation and strategy for organizations or industries.

Now that we understand the various levels of CSA experience, let us learn about compensation expectations for the role of CSA for each level.

Understanding the market and your worth

As of 2023, the current job market for a CSA in the United States still looks promising from an average compensation perspective. Your level, skills, experience, and achievements in cloud computing, as well as the market supply and demand for your role, will determine your actual CSA compensation. To know the market and know your worth, you need to understand what expectations you can have at the junior, senior, and principal levels by region in the United States.

It is important to understand that total compensation includes more than just the base salary for the role. Also included will be any types of bonuses or benefits extended to the employee via the employer.

According to https://www.glassdoor.com, a junior CSA in the United States earns a total compensation of $127,473 per year on average, with a most likely range of $104,000 to $156,000 per year. However, this will likely vary by region, as shown in *Figure 6.1*:

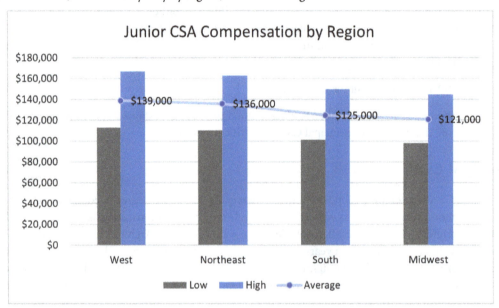

Figure 6.1 – Junior CSA compensation by region

As indicated in the preceding chart, the **West** region of the United States offers the highest average total compensation at **$139,000**, while the **Midwest** region offers the lowest for a junior-level CSA at **$121,000**.

Now that we have seen the pay range for a junior CSA, let us look at the senior level.

Again, according to https://www.glassdoor.com, a senior CSA in the United States tends to earn roughly $191,746 in total compensation. This is a considerable step up from the average compensation for a junior CSA. With more responsibility and experience comes more money for the senior CSA role. The range for the senior role is roughly $150,000 to $250,000 per year. These numbers will also vary by location in the United States, as indicated in *Figure 6.2*:

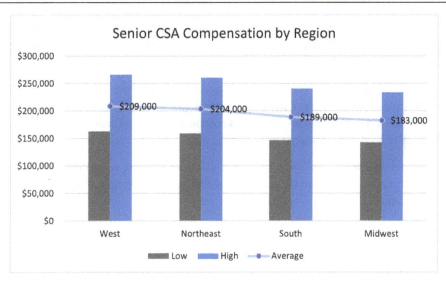

Figure 6.2 – Senior CSA compensation by region

As per the preceding chart, the **West** region of the United States offers the highest average total compensation for a senior CSA at **$209,000**, while the **Midwest** region again offers the lowest for a senior-level CSA at **$183,000**.

Now that we have seen the pay range for a senior CSA, let us look at the principal level.

For the principal CSA role, `https://www.glassdoor.com` was used again as a source of total compensation numbers. A principal CSA in the United States earns $246,486 per year on average. The range for a principal CSA is approximately $193,000 to $323,000. These numbers will also vary by region like the junior and senior levels, as shown in *Figure 6.3*:

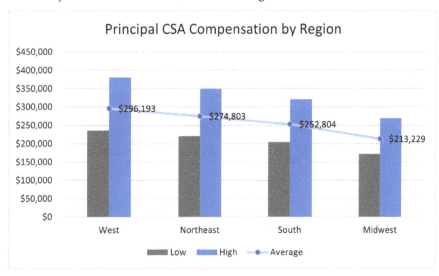

Figure 6.3 – Principal CSA compensation by region

As displayed in the preceding chart, the **West** region of the United States offers the highest average total compensation of **$296,193**, while the **Midwest** region offers the lowest for a principal-level CSA at **$213,229**.

While the aforementioned figures reflect the average compensation per region, there are various factors that will influence the salary of the CSA role, either positively or negatively. Overall supply and demand for CSAs, specific skillsets needed, and economic conditions are examples of factors that can and likely will influence the compensation package offered to a job candidate seeking a CSA role.

At this point, experience levels have been described and compensation ranges have been explored. Now, let us turn our attention toward the primary tool that gets the attention of recruiters and hiring managers: the resume.

Making your resume stand out

Your resume is a document that shows your skills, experience, and achievements in cloud computing to potential employers, hiring managers, and recruiters. To make your resume stand out from the crowd, you should optimize each of the following sections: summary, skills, achievements, and relevancy. Let us start with the resume's summary.

Summary section

Your **summary** is the first thing that a reader will see on your resume, so it needs to be concise, clear, and compelling. It should highlight your most relevant and impressive qualifications for the CSA role, such as your certifications, years of experience, areas of expertise, and career goals. You should use phrases instead of full sentences to keep it short, and tailor it to the specific job posting as much as possible.

Here is an example of a good summary for a CSA resume:

> *AWS Certified Solutions Architect with 5+ years of experience in cloud infrastructure design, security, and migration. Led a team of Cloud Engineers to design a cloud infrastructure and migrated data from legacy systems to increase system availability by 25%. Seeking to apply proven data analysis and programming skills in helping [Target Employer] modernize its extensive data-storage and serving platforms.*

Once the summary is optimized for the specific opportunity, next comes the skills section of the resume.

Skills section

Your **skills** section should list the technical and soft skills that you have acquired and developed as a CSA. Technical skills are the specific knowledge and abilities that you need to perform your job, such as cloud computing platforms, software engineering tools, system design and architecture methods, and analytics techniques. Soft skills are the personal attributes and behaviors that enable you to work effectively with others, such as communication, teamwork, problem-solving, and leadership. You should use industry-relevant keywords that match the job description and organize them into categories or bullet points for easy readability.

Here is an example of a good skills section for a CSA resume:

- *Technical Skills*:

    - *Cloud Computing Platforms*: AWS, Azure, Google Cloud

    - *Software Engineering Tools*: Python, Java, C#, SQL, Git

    - *System Design and Architecture Methods*: UML, RESTful API, microservices

    - *Analytics Techniques*: Data mining, machine learning, visualization

- *Soft Skills*:

    - *Communication*: Written and verbal communication skills with technical and non-technical audiences

    - *Teamwork*: Collaborated with cross-functional teams of developers, testers, analysts, and managers

    - *Problem-Solving*: Analyzed customer requirements and proposed optimal cloud solutions

    - *Leadership*: Mentored junior CSAs and led cloud projects from inception to completion

Skills are important, so make sure enough time is spent documenting those that are associated with the position.

After skills have been assessed, consider the achievements section of the resume.

Achievements section

Your **achievements** section should showcase the results and outcomes that you have delivered as a CSA. Achievements are different from responsibilities or duties in that they demonstrate the impact and value you've broughtto your previous or current employers or clients. You should quantify your achievements using numbers or metrics whenever possible, such as percentages, amounts, or frequencies. You should also use action verbs that highlight your skills and abilities, such as design, implement, improve, or increase.

Here is an example of a good achievements section for a CSA resume:

- *Achievements*:

  - Designed and implemented a complex cloud solution for a large e-commerce company using AWS services such as EC2, S3, RDS, Lambda, and CloudFormation

  - Improved the security and compliance of the cloud infrastructure by implementing encryption, authentication, authorization, logging, and auditing features

  - Migrated over 3 PB of sensitive data from on-premise servers to the cloud using AWS Snowball devices and AWS Data Pipeline

  - Increased the performance and scalability of the cloud infrastructure by optimizing the load balancing, caching, auto-scaling, and monitoring features

The important thing to remember about achievements is to always tie individual achievements to business impact outcomes. This clearly demonstrates the value of the achievement and the importance of the candidate's involvement.

As the resume nears completion, it is important to review the document for relevancy to the role being applied for.

Relevancy section

Relevancy is not a section but rather a goal of a good resume. The application should demonstrate how your skills and experience match the specific requirements and expectations of the CSA role that you are applying for. Relevancy is important because it shows that you have done your research on the position, and that you understand the company's needs and goals. You can increase your relevancy by customizing your resume for each job application using the following tips:

- Use keywords from the job description throughout your resume

- Highlight the projects or tasks that are most similar or relevant to the job description

- Emphasize the skills and achievements that are most valuable or desirable for the job description presented by the potential employer

- Align your career goals or objectives with the company's vision or mission

Again, the important takeaway is to tailor the resume to a specific role or job description to make the content as relevant as possible to the job.

While we're considering a resume that stands out, social media should also be refreshed to be current, impactful, and relevant to the role being pursued. Let us now look at some recommendations for updating social media sites and online profiles.

Updating social media sites

Social media sites are powerful tools for building your personal brand, showcasing your skills and achievements, and connecting with potential employers and recruiters. When you are getting ready to apply for jobs as a CSA, you should update your social media profiles to reflect your status, goals, and qualifications. The following subsections share some recommendations on what to update on the most popular social media platforms.

LinkedIn

LinkedIn (`https://www.linkedin.com`) is the most widely used professional networking site, where you can create and maintain your online resume, portfolio, and network.

You should update your LinkedIn profile with the following information:

- *Your headline*: This is the first thing that people see when they visit your profile, so it should be catchy, concise, and relevant. You should include your current or desired job title, such as *Cloud Solution Architect*, *Senior Cloud Engineer*, or *AWS Certified Solutions Architect*. You should also include some keywords or phrases that highlight your skills or specialties, such as *Cloud Computing*, *AWS*, *Azure*, or *Google Cloud*.

- *Your summary*: This is the second thing that people see when they visit your profile, so it should be clear, compelling, and comprehensive. You should summarize your professional background, experience, and achievements in cloud computing, as well as your career goals and interests. You should also include a call to action, such as inviting people to connect with you, view your portfolio, or contact you regarding opportunities.

- *Your experience*: This is where you list your current and previous jobs, projects, or roles related to cloud computing. You should include the name of the company or organization, the dates of employment or involvement, the job title or role, and a brief description of your responsibilities and accomplishments. You should use bullet points and action verbs to highlight your skills and achievements and quantify them with numbers or metrics whenever possible.

- *Your education*: This is where you list your academic credentials related to cloud computing. You should include the name of the institution, the dates of attendance or graduation, the degree or certificate obtained, and the field of study or major. You should also include any relevant courses, projects, or honors that demonstrate your knowledge and skills in cloud computing.

- *Your skills*: This is where you list your technical and soft skills related to cloud computing. You should include both hard skills, such as cloud computing platforms, software engineering tools, system design and architecture methods, and analytics techniques, and soft skills, such as communication, teamwork, problem-solving, and leadership. You should also endorse and get endorsed by other people for your skills to increase your credibility and visibility.

- *Your certifications*: This is where you list your professional certifications related to cloud computing. You should include the name of the certification provider, such as AWS, Azure, Google Cloud, or Cisco, the name of the certification itself, such as *AWS Certified Solutions Architect - Associate* or *Microsoft Certified: Azure Solutions Architect Expert*, and the date of completion or expiration. You should also upload a copy of your certification badge or certificate to verify your credentials.

Twitter

Twitter (`https://www.twitter.com`), now known as X, is a popular microblogging site where you can share short messages, links, images, videos, and other content with your followers and the public.

You should update your Twitter profile with the following information:

- *Your name*: This is how people identify you on Twitter, so it should be consistent with your real name or professional alias. You should use proper capitalization and punctuation to make it easy to read and remember.

- *Your username*: This is how people find you on Twitter, so it should be unique, memorable, and relevant. You should use a combination of letters and numbers that reflects your name or profession. For example, you could use *@CloudArchitect*, *@AWS_Solutions*, or *@Azure_Expert*.

- *Your bio*: This is where you describe yourself in 160 characters or less, so it should be concise, catchy, and informative. You should include some keywords or hashtags that relate to your profession or interests in cloud computing. For example, you could use *#CloudSolutionArchitect*, *#AWS*, *#Azure*, *#GoogleCloud*, or *#CloudComputing*.

- *Your location*: This is where you indicate where you are based or where you are willing to work. You should use a city name or a region name that is recognizable and relevant. For example, you could use *San Francisco*, *New York*, *London*, *Singapore*, or *Remote*.

- *Your website*: This is where you provide a link to your online portfolio, resume, blog, or other website that showcases your work and skills in cloud computing. You should use a short and simple URL that is easy to type and remember.

GitHub

GitHub (`https://www.github.com`) is a leading platform for hosting and collaborating on software development projects using the Git version control system. GitHub is widely used by developers and engineers who work with cloud computing platforms and tools.

You should update your GitHub profile with the following information:

- *Your name*: This is how people identify you on GitHub, so it should be consistent with your real name or professional alias. You should use proper capitalization and punctuation to make it easy to read and remember.

- *Your username*: This is how people find you on GitHub, so it should be unique, memorable, and relevant. You should use a combination of letters and numbers that reflects your name or profession. For example, you could use *CloudArchitect*, *AWS-Solutions*, or *Azure-Expert*.

- *Your bio*: This is where you describe yourself in 160 characters or less, so it should be concise, catchy, and informative. You should include some keywords or phrases that relate to your profession or interests in cloud computing. For example, you could use *Cloud Solution Architect*, *AWS*, *Azure*, *Google Cloud*, or *Cloud Computing*.

- *Your location*: This is where you indicate where you are based or where you are willing to work. You should use a city name or a region name that is recognizable and relevant. For example, you could use *San Francisco*, *New York*, *London*, *Singapore*, or *Remote*.

- *Your website*: This is where you provide a link to your online portfolio, resume, blog, or other website that showcases your work and skills in cloud computing. You should use a short and simple URL that is easy to type and remember.

- *Your repositories*: These are where you store and manage your code and projects related to cloud computing. You should create and update your repositories regularly with clear and descriptive names, README files, comments, documentation, and licenses. You should also showcase your best or most recent projects by pinning them to your profile page.

- *Your contributions*: These are the places where you show your activity and involvement in cloud computing projects on GitHub. You should contribute to your own or other people's repositories by creating issues, pull requests, commits, forks, stars, and reviews. You should also participate in discussions and feed back on cloud computing topics by commenting on issues, pull requests, and forums.

Medium

Medium (`https://www.medium.com`) is a popular online publishing platform where you can write and share articles, stories, tutorials, guides, and other content with a large and engaged audience. Medium is a great way to demonstrate your knowledge and expertise in cloud computing, as well as to learn from other experts and influencers in the field.

You should update your Medium profile with the following information:

- *Your name*: This is how people identify you on Medium, so it should be consistent with your real name or professional alias. You should use proper capitalization and punctuation to make it easy to read and remember.

- *Your username*: This is how people find you on Medium, so it should be unique, memorable, and relevant. You should use a combination of letters and numbers that reflects your name or profession. For example, you could use *@CloudArchitect*, *@AWS_Solutions*, or *@Azure_Expert*.

- *Your bio*: This is where you describe yourself in 160 characters or less, so it should be concise, catchy, and informative. You should include some keywords or phrases that relate to your profession or interests in cloud computing. For example, you could use *Cloud Solution Architect*, *AWS*, *Azure*, *Google Cloud*, or *Cloud Computing*.

- *Your location*: This is where you indicate where you are based or where you are willing to work. You should use a city name or a region name that is recognizable and relevant. For example, you could use *San Francisco*, *New York*, *London*, *Singapore*, or *Remote*.

- *Your website*: This is where you provide a link to your online portfolio, resume, blog, or other website that showcases your work and skills in cloud computing. You should use a short and simple URL that is easy to type and remember.

- *Your stories*: This is where you write and share your articles, stories, tutorials, guides, and other content related to cloud computing. You should write and publish your stories regularly with clear and engaging titles, subtitles, images, tags, and links. You should also follow the best practices for writing on Medium, such as using headings, lists, quotes, code blocks, embeds, formatting, grammar, spelling, and style.

- *Your publications*: These are the topics you join or create from collections of stories related to cloud computing topics or themes. You should join or create publications that are relevant and reputable in the cloud computing community. You should also follow the guidelines and rules for each publication, such as submitting quality content, respecting the editorial process, crediting the sources, and engaging with the readers.

Now that we've explored social media and how it can be used as a tool in the pursuit of a career as a CSA, let us look at other preparatory work to be completed before the interview process that will help CSA candidates be as effective as possible in the actual interview.

Preparing interview questions

At the end of the interview, there will likely be a chance to ask some questions of the people conducting it. This is a chance to show curiosity and enthusiasm for the job and clarify any doubts or concerns. Some more usual questions that are relevant and insightful, such as the following:

- What are some of the current or upcoming cloud projects or initiatives that you are working on or planning to work on?

- What are some of the best practices or standards that you follow or recommend for cloud solutions architecture?

- What are some of the tools or resources that you use or provide for learning and development in cloud computing?

- How do you measure or evaluate the success or impact of cloud solutions?

- What are some of the challenges or difficulties that you face or anticipate in cloud computing?

- How would you describe the culture or work environment of your team or organization?

The preceding list of questions gives examples of extremely broad topics that are applicable to almost every interview scenario. In addition to these, it will be important to understand the industry related to the job opening to be able to ask more specific questions. For example, in the automotive industry, a good question for a job interview might be something similar to "What are the regulatory requirements related to architectures developed for vehicle telemetry communications and how do they affect any architectural decisions a CSA may propose?"

Deciding on the experience level desired, being aware of the current job market and CSA compensation ranges, having an impactful resume and fresh social media content, and being prepared to ask relevant questions will put a candidate in an ideal position for the interview process. Let us now summarize more specifically what was covered in this chapter, and what we can expect to learn in the next chapter.

Summary

In this chapter, you learned how to define your level of experience and responsibility as a CSA. You learned that a CSA can be classified as junior, senior, or principal, depending on their level of experience and responsibility. Each level has different roles and expectations, as well as different salary ranges and career paths. You learned what qualifications you need to have for each level.

The next thing you learned was how to understand your salary expectations as a CSA. You learned that your skills, experience, and achievements in cloud computing, as well as the market demand and supply for your role, determine your CSA salary. You learned what salary expectations you can have at each level by region in the United States, based on the average total pay and the most likely range from various sources.

The third thing you learned was how to optimize your resume as a CSA. You learned how to draw attention to your resume for each of the following sections: summary, skills, achievements, and overall relevancy of the resume. You learned how to showcase your results and outcomes that demonstrate your impact and value as a CSA and quantify them using numbers or metrics. You learned how to demonstrate how your skills and experience match the specific requirements and expectations of the CSA role that you are applying for and customize your resume for each job application.

Next, we talked about recommendations to update a social media presence. Social media sites are powerful tools for building your personal brand, showcasing your skills and achievements, and connecting with potential employers and recruiters. In this section, you learned how to update your social media profiles on LinkedIn, Twitter, GitHub, and Medium to reflect your current status, goals, and qualifications as a CSA. You learned what information to include and how to present it in a clear, compelling, and relevant way. You also learned how to use keywords, hashtags, links, images, tags, and other features to increase your visibility and credibility in the cloud computing community.

Finally, we explored broad interview questions that a candidate can ask of the interviewers to express an understanding of the job duties, and discussed the need to ask industry-specific questions to demonstrate a genuine interest and enthusiasm for the role.

Now that we have done the preparation for a job interview, let us turn our attention to the interviewing process in the next chapter.

Additional resources

For further consideration, the following list provides additional resources that can help supplement the content of this chapter:

- *Seniority Levels in the Workplace: Types and What They Mean*: This article on `Indeed.com` provides an overview of seniority levels in the workplace, including junior, senior, and principal roles. It explains what seniority is, how it can influence your career, and its impact on the workplace: `https://www.indeed.com/career-advice/career-development/seniority-level`.

- *CSA Resume Sample*: This article by CV Owl provides a sample CSA resume and tips on how to make your resume stand out: `https://www.cvowl.com/resume-sample/csa`.

- *How to Spring Clean Your Social Media Platforms (and Make Them Recruiter-Ready)*: This article by The Muse provides guidance on how often you should update your social media platforms to make them recruiter-ready: `https://www.themuse.com/advice/how-to-spring-clean-your-social-media-platforms-and-make-them-recruiterready`.

- *6 Essential Networking Sites for Social Media Recruiting*: This article by HR Daily Advisor lists six essential networking sites for social media recruiting: `https://hrdailyadvisor.blr.com/2017/02/14/6-essential-networking-sites-social-media-recruiting/`.

7

Interviewing – Trust the Process

Once you are ready to seek employment, interviewing as a process is straightforward. In this chapter, you will learn how to prepare for and ace an interview. You will also discover some common questions and scenarios that you might face in a **cloud solution architect** (**CSA**) interview and how to answer them effectively and confidently.

To help you achieve these objectives, this chapter will guide you through two main aspects of the interview preparation process: practicing and answering. In the first section, we will discuss why practicing is important, how to practice effectively, and which resources and tools you can use to enhance your learning and performance. In the second section, we will provide some examples of common questions and scenarios that you might encounter in a CSA interview and give you some tips on how to answer them.

By the end of this chapter, you will be able to prepare for a CSA interview in a comprehensive and systematic way. You will also be able to emphasize your skills and knowledge, impress your interviewer, and land your dream job.

This content will be provided via the following topics in the chapter:

- Interview success strategies
- Common questions and scenarios worth preparing for

Let us begin by exploring ways to practice for an upcoming interview and how to be as prepared as possible.

Interview success strategies

One of the most crucial steps to prepare for a CSA interview is to practice your skills and knowledge. Practicing will help you to improve your confidence, communication, and problem-solving abilities. It will also help you to identify your strengths and weaknesses and work on them accordingly.

There are different ways to practice for an interview, depending on your goals and preferences. Here are some suggestions:

- *Practice with yourself*: The best way to practice for an interview is to combine different methods and sources of feedback. You should also practice in a realistic setting that simulates the actual interview environment. For example, you should dress professionally, use a clear and reliable microphone and camera, avoid distractions and interruptions, and so on.

- You can practice by yourself by reviewing the concepts and technologies related to cloud solution architecture, such as cloud computing models, **cloud service providers (CSPs)**, cloud design patterns, cloud security, cloud migration, and so on. You can also use online resources such as blogs, podcasts, videos, courses, books, and so on to learn more about the latest trends and best practices in the field. You can also try to solve some mock questions or scenarios that are relevant to the role of CSA. You can find examples of such questions or scenarios on websites such as *Glassdoor* (`https://www.glassdoor.com`), *Indeed* (`https://www.indeed.com/`), or *LeetCode* (`https://www.leetcode.com/`).

- *Practice with a friend or a mentor*: You can practice with a friend or a mentor who has experience or interest in cloud solution architecture. You can ask them to give you feedback on your answers, presentation, and attitude. You can also ask them to challenge you with some difficult or unexpected questions or scenarios that might come up in an interview. You can also exchange roles and try to interview them as well.

- *Practice with an online platform or a community*: You can practice with an online platform or a community that offers mock interviews or peer-to-peer feedback for cloud solution architecture. You can find some examples of such platforms or communities on websites such as *Pramp* (`https://www.pramp.com/`), *Interview Cake* (`https://www.interviewcake.com/`), or *Interviewing.io* (`https://www.interviewing.io/`). You can also join some online forums or groups where you can interact with other CSAs or aspirants and learn from their experiences and insights.

- *Practice with a professional or a recruiter*: You can practice with a professional or a recruiter who has expertise or connections in the field of cloud solution architecture. You can ask them to conduct a mock interview for you and give you constructive criticism and tips on how to improve your performance and chances of getting hired. You can also ask them to refer you to some potential employers or opportunities that match your profile and goals.

- *Prepare a list of technologies*: Prepare a list of cloud provider platform technologies that have been previously used in successful workload deployments. This list can be compared against jobs posted to ensure a cursory match with existing skill sets and experience.

Practicing for an interview is not only beneficial for your technical skills and knowledge but also for your mental and emotional well-being. It will help you to reduce your stress and anxiety levels, boost your self-esteem and motivation, and increase your enthusiasm and passion for the role of CSA.

In summary, practicing for an interview is an essential part of preparing for a career as a CSA. It will help you to highlight your skills and knowledge, impress your interviewer, and land your dream job. In the next section, we will discuss some common questions and scenarios that you might encounter in a CSA interview. We will also provide some tips on how to answer these questions effectively and confidently.

Common questions and scenarios worth preparing for

The following list of example questions can occur for any level of experience within a CSA job interview. As will be seen, some questions are targeted toward a general understanding of the various cloud models, while others target more advanced scenarios, such as designing a scalable and resilient cloud architecture. In the absence of direct experience related to the question, it will still help you stand out to be able to address the question with a potential solution, based on what you know.

In all the following examples, it should be noticed that the answers follow the STAR method. The **STAR method** is a technique that can help you structure your answers in a clear and effective way. It stands for **Situation, Task, Action, and Result**. The STAR method can help you provide specific examples and evidence to support your claims and demonstrate your skills and knowledge.

Let us begin with some of the more common questions that come up when interviewing for a CSA role, whether the role is a junior, senior, or principal CSA. Before reading each answer to the questions listed, pause and draft your own response. Then, compare the response with the answer in the text to see how they compare in completeness and clarity.

What experience do you have with designing and implementing cloud-based solutions?

This is a general question that aims to assess your background, experience, and achievements in cloud computing. You should answer this question by briefly summarizing your professional history, highlighting projects or tasks that are most relevant or impressive for the CSA role, and describing cloud platforms, tools, methods, and techniques that you used or learned. You should also mention any certifications, awards, or recognitions that you have obtained or received in cloud computing. Here is an example of a good answer:

Sample answer: I have over 5 years of experience as a cloud engineer and a CSA, working with various cloud platforms such as AWS, Azure, and Google Cloud. I have designed and implemented cloud solutions for different use cases and industries, such as e-commerce, healthcare, education, and finance. Specific projects that I am most proud of are the following:

- Designing and implementing a scalable and secure cloud infrastructure for an online shopping platform using AWS services such as EC2, S3, RDS, Lambda, and CloudFormation

- Migrating from a legacy healthcare system from on-premise servers to the Azure cloud using the Azure Migrate tool and the Azure DevOps service

- Developing a cloud-native web application for an online learning platform using Google Cloud services such as App Engine, Cloud Storage, Cloud SQL, Cloud Functions, and Firebase

- Optimizing the performance and cost efficiency of a cloud-based financial system using various cloud computing techniques such as load balancing, caching, auto-scaling, monitoring, and auditing

I have also obtained several professional certifications in cloud computing, such as *AWS Certified Solutions Architect - Professional, Microsoft Certified: Azure Solutions Architect Expert2*, and *Google Certified Professional Cloud Architect*. In addition, I have received several awards and recognitions from my previous employers and clients for my outstanding work and contributions to cloud computing.

Describe a time when you had to fix an issue with a cloud-based workload

This is a behavioral question that aims to evaluate your problem-solving skills and your ability to handle challenges or difficulties in cloud computing. You should answer this question by using the **STAR** method. You should describe a specific situation where you faced an issue with a cloud-based system, explain the task or goal that you had to achieve or accomplish, describe the actions or steps that you took to troubleshoot or resolve the issue, and state the result or outcome that you achieved or accomplished. You should also mention any lessons learned or improvements made from the experience. Here is an example of a good answer:

Sample answer: A situation where I had to troubleshoot an issue with a cloud-based system was when I was working as a cloud engineer for an e-commerce company. The company had a web application hosted on AWS EC2 instances that allowed customers to browse and purchase products online. The task was to ensure that the web application was running smoothly and securely without any downtime or errors.

One day, I noticed that the web application was experiencing slow response times and frequent timeouts. This was affecting the customer experience and the sales performance of the company. The action that I took was to investigate the root cause of the issue using various tools and methods such as Amazon CloudWatch, AWS X-Ray ping tests, traceroute tests, log analysis, and code review. I found out that the issue was caused by a network latency problem between the EC2 instances and the Amazon RDS database that stored the product information. The network latency problem was due to a misconfiguration of the security groups and subnets that controlled the network access between the EC2 instances and the RDS database.

The result was that I fixed the issue by reconfiguring the security groups and subnets to allow optimal network connectivity between the EC2 instances and the RDS database. I also tested the web application to ensure that it was working properly and efficiently without any delays or failures. I also documented the issue and the solution for future reference and improvement.

The lesson learned from this experience was that network latency can have a significant impact on the performance and reliability of cloud-based systems. Therefore, it is important to monitor and optimize the network configuration and access between different cloud components to ensure optimal performance and reliability.

How familiar are you with the different types of cloud computing services?

This is a technical question that aims to assess your knowledge and understanding of the different types of cloud computing services and how they are used or applied in different scenarios and domains. You should answer this question by briefly explaining the meaning and characteristics of each type of cloud computing service, such as **Infrastructure as a Service (IaaS)**, **Platform as a Service (PaaS)**, and **Software as a Service (SaaS)**. You should also provide some examples of each type of cloud computing service from different cloud providers, such as AWS, Azure, or Google Cloud. Here is an example of a good answer:

Sample answer: I am familiar with the different types of cloud computing services and how they are used or applied in different scenarios and domains. The different types of cloud computing services are the following:

- *Hybrid*: A hybrid cloud solution is a combination of environments, usually consisting of on-premises and cloud provider locations that work together to provide flexibility, scalability, and redundancy for business workloads.

- *IaaS*: This is a type of cloud computing service that provides basic computing resources, such as servers, storage, network, and virtualization, that users can rent and use on demand. Users have full control and responsibility over the configuration and management of these resources.

- *PaaS*: This is a type of cloud computing service that provides the development and deployment environment, such as operating system, programming language, framework, middleware, and tools, that users can use to create and run applications on the cloud. Users have less control and responsibility over the configuration and management of these resources as the cloud provider handles them.

- *SaaS*: This is a type of cloud computing service that provides ready-made applications, such as email, **customer relationship management (CRM)**, **enterprise resource planning** (ERP), or collaboration, that users can access and use over the internet. Users have no control or responsibility over the configuration and management of these resources as the cloud provider handles them.

What are some of the benefits and drawbacks of cloud computing?

This is a technical question that aims to assess your knowledge and understanding of the pros and cons of cloud computing and how they affect different scenarios and domains. You should answer this question by briefly explaining the meaning and scope of cloud computing, identifying the main benefits and drawbacks of cloud computing, such as scalability, flexibility, reliability, security, and cost efficiency, and describing how they apply to or impact different use cases and industries. You should also provide some examples or scenarios that illustrate the benefits and drawbacks of cloud computing. Here is an example of a good answer:

Sample answer: Cloud computing is the delivery of computing services, such as servers, storage, network, software, and applications, over the internet, without the need for expensive and complex hardware and software. Cloud computing offers many benefits and drawbacks for different use cases and industries. Some of the benefits and drawbacks of cloud computing are the following:

- *Scalability*: This is the ability to increase or decrease the amount of resources or services according to the demand or workload. Scalability is a benefit of cloud computing because it allows users to adjust their resources or services dynamically and efficiently without wasting time or money. Scalability is also a drawback of cloud computing because it can introduce complexity and unpredictability in managing and monitoring resources or services. For example, a benefit of scalability is that an e-commerce company can scale up its web application during peak seasons or events to handle more traffic and transactions. A drawback of scalability is that a healthcare company may face challenges in scaling down its data processing system after a surge in patient records.

- *Flexibility*: This is the ability to choose or customize resources or services according to needs or preferences. Flexibility is a benefit of cloud computing because it allows users to select or modify their resources or services from a variety of options and features without being limited by physical or technical constraints. Flexibility is also a drawback of cloud computing because it can introduce compatibility and compliance issues in integrating and using different resources or services. For example, a benefit of flexibility is that an education company can choose or customize its learning platform from different cloud providers, such as AWS, Azure, or Google Cloud. A drawback of flexibility is that a finance company may face difficulties in complying with different regulations and standards when using different cloud services.

- *Reliability*: This is the ability to ensure the availability and performance of resources or services without interruption or failure. Reliability is a benefit of cloud computing because it allows users to access and use their resources or services anytime and anywhere without worrying about downtime or errors. Reliability is also a drawback of cloud computing because it can introduce dependency and vulnerability in relying on external parties or factors for maintaining and securing resources or services. For example, a benefit of reliability is that a media company can stream its content to its customers around the world without interruption or failure. A drawback of reliability is that a government agency may lose access to its data or applications if the cloud provider experiences an outage or an attack.

- *Security*: This is the protection of data and resources from unauthorized access or modification. Security is a benefit of cloud computing because it allows users to leverage the expertise and technology of the cloud provider to safeguard their data and resources without investing in expensive and complex security measures. Security is also a drawback of cloud computing because it can introduce risk and responsibility in sharing or transferring data and resources to external parties or locations. For example, a benefit of security is that a research company can encrypt and back up its data on the cloud without buying and maintaining encryption and backup devices. A common drawback of security is enterprises taking the position that securing the cloud is like securing the data center and not taking advantage of modern cloud security practices such as using identity as a perimeter rather than just a traditional network firewall.

- *Cost efficiency*: This is the reduction of expenses or waste in using or consuming resources or services. Cost efficiency is a benefit of cloud computing because it allows users to pay only for what they use or need without incurring spend on unnecessary or unused resources or services. Cost efficiency is also a drawback of cloud computing because it can introduce unpredictability and complexity in estimating and managing the costs of using or consuming resources or services. For example, a benefit of cost efficiency is that a start-up company can launch its product on the cloud with minimal upfront costs without buying or renting hardware or software. A drawback of cost efficiency is that an enterprise company may incur unexpected or hidden costs on the cloud due to variable usage patterns, service fees, taxes, or currency fluctuations.

How do you design a scalable and resilient cloud architecture?

This is a technical question that aims to evaluate your skills and abilities in designing a scalable and resilient cloud architecture for different use cases and industries. You should answer this question by briefly explaining the meaning and importance of scalability and resilience for cloud-based systems. This should include identifying the main principles or factors for designing a scalable and resilient cloud architecture, such as modularity, redundancy, load balancing, auto-scaling, **fault tolerance** (**FT**), or **disaster recovery** (**DR**). The answer should also include describing the main steps or processes for designing a scalable and resilient cloud architecture, such as defining the requirements, selecting components, configuring parameters, testing the functionality, and monitoring performance. You should also provide some examples or diagrams that illustrate the design of a scalable and resilient cloud architecture. Here is an example of a good answer:

Sample answer: Scalability is the ability to increase or decrease the amount of resources or services according to the demand or workload. Resilience is the ability to ensure the availability and performance of resources or services without interruption or failure. Scalability and resilience are important for cloud-based systems because they ensure the optimal and reliable delivery of computing services to users and stakeholders in the cloud.

Some of the main principles or factors for designing a scalable and resilient cloud architecture are the following:

- *Modularity*: This is the principle of dividing a system into smaller and independent units or modules that can communicate and interact with each other. Modularity enables scalability and resilience by allowing easy addition or removal of modules, as well as isolation and containment of failures.

- *Redundancy*: This is the principle of duplicating or replicating resources or services to provide backup or alternative options in case of failure or unavailability. Redundancy enables scalability and resilience by allowing load distribution or failover among multiple resources or services.

- *Load balancing*: This is the principle of distributing or balancing the workload or traffic among multiple resources or services to optimize their utilization and performance. Load balancing enables scalability and resilience by allowing dynamic allocation or reallocation of workloads or traffic based on demand or availability.

- *Auto-scaling*: This is the principle of automatically adjusting the amount of resources or services based on predefined rules or metrics. Auto-scaling enables scalability and resilience by allowing elastic scaling up or down of resources or services based on demand or workload.

- *FT*: This is the principle of detecting and handling errors or failures in resources or services without affecting their functionality or performance. FT enables scalability and resilience by allowing graceful degradation or recovery of resources or services in case of errors or failures.

- *DR*: This is the principle of restoring or recovering the functionality or performance of resources or services after a major disruption or catastrophe. DR enables scalability and resilience by allowing backup or restore of data or applications in case of disasters.

Some of the main steps or processes for designing a scalable and resilient cloud architecture are the following:

- *Defining the requirements*: This is the step of identifying and specifying the functional and non-functional requirements for the system, such as the objectives, scope, features, constraints, assumptions, dependencies, or risks

- *Selecting components*: This is the step of choosing and selecting appropriate cloud components that meet the requirements for the system, such as the cloud platform, service model, deployment model, **service provider (SP)**, **service-level agreement (SLA)**, or cost model

- *Configuring parameters*: This is the step of setting and adjusting parameters that control the behavior and performance of cloud components, such as security groups, subnets, load balancers, auto-scaling groups, FT mechanisms, DR strategies, or cost optimization techniques

- *Testing the functionality*: This is the step of verifying and validating that cloud components function correctly and efficiently according to the requirements of the system, such as using unit testing, integration testing, system testing, performance testing, security testing, usability testing, or acceptance testing

- *Monitoring performance*: This is the step of measuring and evaluating that cloud components perform optimally and reliably according to the requirements of the system, such as using metrics, logs, alerts, dashboards, reports, or feedback

What are some best practices for optimizing cloud costs?

This is a technical question that aims to assess your knowledge and understanding of how to optimize cloud costs for different use cases and industries. You should answer this question by briefly explaining what cloud costs are and why they are important to optimize them, identifying some of the main factors that affect cloud costs, such as resource usage, service fees, taxes, or currency fluctuations, and describing some of the best practices for optimizing cloud costs, such as resource planning, resource allocation, resource utilization, resource monitoring, resource optimization, or resource governance. You should also provide some examples of tools or methods that help you optimize cloud costs, such as AWS Cost Explorer, Azure Cost Management, Google Cloud Billing, or Cloudability. Here is an example of a good answer:

Sample answer: Cloud costs are expenses incurred by using cloud computing services, such as servers, storage, network, software, and applications, over time. Cloud costs are important to optimize because they affect the profitability and sustainability of cloud-based systems. Cloud costs are also important to optimize because they reflect the efficiency and effectiveness of cloud computing services.

Some main factors that affect cloud costs are the following:

- *Resource usage*: This is the amount or volume of resources or services that are used or consumed by a system over time. Resource usage affects cloud costs because it determines how much users pay for using or consuming resources or services in the cloud. For example, more resource usage means more cloud costs.

- *Service fees*: This is the amount or rate of fees that are charged by the cloud provider for providing or delivering resources or services in the cloud. Service fees affect cloud costs because they add to the expenses of using or consuming resources or services in the cloud. For example, higher service fees mean higher cloud costs.

- *Taxes*: This is the amount or percentage of taxes that are imposed by the government or authority for using or consuming resources or services in the cloud. Taxes affect cloud costs because they increase the expenses of using or consuming resources or services in the cloud. For example, more taxes mean more cloud costs.

- *Currency fluctuations*: This is the change or variation of currency values or exchange rates between different countries or regions for using or consuming resources or services in the cloud. Currency fluctuations affect cloud costs because they alter the expenses of using or consuming resources or services in the cloud. For example, unfavorable currency fluctuations mean higher cloud costs.

Some best practices for optimizing cloud costs are the following:

- *Resource planning*: This is the practice of identifying and estimating the resource needs and demands for a system before using or consuming resources or services in the cloud. Resource planning helps optimize cloud costs by allowing users to budget and allocate their resources or services in advance without overspending or underutilizing them.

- *Resource allocation*: This is the practice of assigning and distributing resources or services to a system according to its needs and demands while using or consuming resources or services in the cloud. Resource allocation helps optimize cloud costs by allowing users to balance and optimize their resource utilization and performance without wasting or depleting them.

- *Resource utilization*: This is the practice of measuring and monitoring how well or poorly a system uses or consumes resources or services in the cloud. Resource utilization helps optimize cloud costs by allowing users to analyze and improve their resource efficiency and effectiveness without compromising or sacrificing them.

- *Resource monitoring*: This is the practice of tracking and reporting the status and performance of resources or services in a system while using or consuming resources or services in the cloud. Resource monitoring helps optimize cloud costs by allowing users to detect and resolve any issues or problems with their resources or services, such as errors, failures, bottlenecks, spikes, or anomalies.

- *Resource optimization*: This is the practice of adjusting and improving the configuration and management of resources or services in a system while using or consuming resources or services in the cloud. Resource optimization helps optimize cloud costs by allowing users to reduce and eliminate any unnecessary or unused resources or services, such as idle instances, orphaned volumes, outdated snapshots, duplicate data, or redundant backups.

- *Resource governance*: This is the practice of establishing and enforcing policies and rules for using and consuming resources or services in a system while using or consuming resources or services in the cloud. Resource governance helps optimize cloud costs by allowing users to control and regulate their resource access and usage, such as setting quotas, limits, permissions, roles, tags, alerts, notifications, or approvals.

Some examples of tools or methods that help you optimize cloud costs are the following:

- *AWS Cost Explorer*: This is a tool that helps you visualize and analyze your AWS spending and usage over time. You can use AWS Cost Explorer to view your AWS bills, cost trends, cost breakdowns, cost forecasts, or cost recommendations.

- *Azure Cost Management*: This is a tool that helps you monitor and optimize your Azure spending and usage over time. You can use Azure Cost Management to view your Azure invoices, cost reports, cost alerts, cost analysis, or cost optimization.

- *Google Cloud Billing*: This is a tool that helps you manage and optimize your Google Cloud spending and usage over time. You can use Google Cloud Billing to view your Google Cloud statements, cost charts, cost tables, cost insights, or cost recommendations.

- *Cloudability*: This is a tool that helps you optimize your cloud spending and usage across multiple cloud providers over time. You can use Cloudability to view your cloud costs, cloud savings, cloud trends, cloud benchmarks, or cloud actions.

Explain your understanding of the security considerations for cloud-based systems

This is a technical question that aims to assess your knowledge and understanding of security considerations for cloud-based systems and how they are addressed or implemented in different scenarios and domains. You should answer this question by briefly explaining the meaning and importance of security for cloud-based systems, identifying the main security challenges or risks for cloud-based systems, such as data breaches, unauthorized access, **denial-of-service** (**DoS**) attacks, or misconfiguration errors, and describing the main security solutions or best practices for cloud-based systems, such as encryption, authentication, authorization, logging, auditing, or backup. You should also provide some examples of security solutions or best practices from different cloud providers, such as AWS, Azure, or Google Cloud. Here is an example of a good answer:

Sample answer: Security is the protection of data and resources from unauthorized access or modification in cloud-based systems. Security is important for cloud-based systems because it ensures the confidentiality, integrity, availability, and compliance of data and resources in the cloud. Security is also important for cloud-based systems because it builds trust and confidence among users and stakeholders in the cloud.

Some of the main security challenges or risks for cloud-based systems are the following:

- *Data breaches*: This is when unauthorized parties gain access to sensitive or confidential data stored in the cloud. Data breaches can result in data loss, data corruption, data leakage, or data theft.

- *Unauthorized access*: This is when unauthorized parties gain access to resources or services in the cloud. Unauthorized access can result in resource abuse, resource depletion, resource damage, or resource hijacking.

- *DoS attacks*: This is when malicious parties overwhelm or disrupt the availability or performance of resources or services in the cloud. DoS attacks can result in resource unavailability, resource slowdowns, and resource failures.

- *Misconfiguration errors*: This is when users or administrators make mistakes or oversights in configuring or managing resources or services in the cloud. Misconfiguration errors can result in security vulnerabilities, security gaps, and security breaches.

Some of the main security solutions or best practices for cloud-based systems are the following:

- *Encryption*: This is when data is transformed into an unreadable form using a secret key or algorithm. Encryption protects data from unauthorized access either in transit or at rest. Some examples of encryption solutions are AWS KMS, Azure Key Vault, and Google Cloud KMS.

- *Authentication*: This is when users or entities prove their identity using credentials such as username/password tokens and certificates. Authentication prevents unauthorized access to resources or services in the cloud. Some examples of authentication solutions are AWS IAM, Azure Active Directory, and Google Cloud Identity.

- *Authorization*: This is when users or entities are granted permission to access or perform actions on resources or services in the cloud based on their roles, policies, and rules. Authorization controls unauthorized access to resources or services in the cloud. Some examples of authorization solutions are AWS IAM policies, Azure RBAC, and Google Cloud IAM.

- *Logging*: This is when users or administrators record and store information about activities and events that occur in resources or services in the cloud. Logging provides visibility and accountability for resources or services in the cloud. Some examples of logging solutions are AWS CloudTrail, Azure Monitor, and Google Cloud Logging.

- *Auditing*: This is when users or administrators review and analyze information recorded and stored by logging solutions to verify and validate the compliance and performance of resources or services in the cloud. Auditing provides assurance and improvement for resources or services in the cloud. Some examples of auditing solutions are AWS Config, Azure Policy, and Google Cloud Security Command Center.

- *Backup*: This is when users or administrators copy and store data from resources or services in the cloud to another location or medium for recovery purposes. Backup protects data from loss or corruption in case of disasters or errors. Some examples of backup solutions are Amazon S3, Azure Backup, and Google Cloud Storage.

Explain some tools or methods used to monitor and optimize performance

This is a technical question that aims to assess your skills and abilities in monitoring and optimizing the performance of cloud-based systems for different use cases and industries. You should answer this question by briefly explaining what performance is and why it is important to monitor and optimize it, identifying some of the main tools or methods that you use to monitor and optimize the performance of cloud-based systems, such as metrics, logs, alerts, dashboards, reports, or feedback, and describing how you use these tools or methods to measure, analyze, improve, or report the performance of cloud-based systems. You should also provide some examples of tools or methods that you use from different cloud providers, such as AWS, Azure, or Google Cloud. Here is an example of a good answer:

Sample answer: Performance is the measure of how well or poorly a system delivers its functionality or service to users or stakeholders in terms of speed, reliability, availability, or quality. Performance is important to monitor and optimize because it affects the user experience and satisfaction, as well as the business outcomes and objectives of cloud-based systems.

Some tools or methods that I use to monitor and optimize the performance of cloud-based systems are the following:

- *Metrics*: These are numerical values that represent the status or behavior of resources or services in a system over time. Metrics help monitor and optimize the performance of cloud-based systems by allowing users to quantify and track their resource utilization and performance, such as CPU usage, memory usage, network throughput, response time, error rate, or availability. Some examples of metrics tools are AWS CloudWatch, Azure Monitor, and Google Cloud Monitoring.

- *Logs*: These are textual records that capture activities and events that occur in resources or services in a system over time. Logs help monitor and optimize the performance of cloud-based systems by allowing users to investigate and troubleshoot any issues or problems with their resources or services, such as errors, failures, bottlenecks, spikes, or anomalies. Some examples of log tools are AWS CloudTrail, Azure Monitor, and Google Cloud Logging.

- *Alerts*: These are notifications that inform users about any changes or deviations in the status or behavior of resources or services in a system over time. Alerts help monitor and optimize the performance of cloud-based systems by allowing users to react and respond quickly to any issues or problems with their resources or services, such as errors, failures, bottlenecks, spikes, or anomalies. Some examples of alert tools are Amazon SNS, Azure Alerts, and Google Cloud Alerting.

- *Dashboards*: These are graphical interfaces that display metrics, logs, alerts, and other information about resources or services in a system over time. Dashboards help monitor and optimize the performance of cloud-based systems by allowing users to visualize and understand their resource utilization and performance, as well as to identify any trends or patterns in their data. Some examples of dashboard tools are AWS CloudFormation, Azure dashboards, and the Google Cloud console.

- *Reports*: These are documents that summarize and analyze metrics, logs, alerts, and other information about resources or services in a system over time. Reports help monitor and optimize the performance of cloud-based systems by allowing users to communicate and share their resource utilization and performance results with other users or stakeholders, as well as to provide recommendations for improvement. Some examples of reporting tools are AWS Cost Explorer, Azure Cost Management, and Google Cloud Billing.

- *Feedback*: This is the input or opinion that users or stakeholders provide about the functionality or service delivered by a system over time. Feedback helps monitor and optimize the performance of cloud-based systems by allowing users to evaluate and improve their user experience and satisfaction as well as their business outcomes and objectives.

As the candidate in the interview process, these questions give you a decent understanding of some basic and advanced questions you are likely to encounter when interviewing for a CSA role. This is by no means an exhaustive list, and as cloud technologies evolve, these questions will likely change. The important takeaway is that being prepared to answer questions from either an experience or a hypothetical perspective will help avoid being caught off guard and not being able to answer a particular question.

Summary

In this chapter, we discussed how to prepare for a CSA interview. We covered two main aspects of the preparation process: practicing and answering.

To cover these topics, we emphasized the importance of practicing for an interview and explained how practicing can help you improve your skills and knowledge, confidence, communication, and problem-solving abilities. Also explored were some common questions and scenarios you might encounter in a CSA interview. We also gave some tips on how to answer them effectively and confidently. By following the advice and guidance given in this chapter, you will be able to prepare for a CSA interview in a comprehensive and systematic way. You will be able to highlight your skills and knowledge, impress your interviewer, and land your dream job.

In the next chapter, we will discuss how to keep your skills current and stay on top of emerging capabilities and trends in the cloud computing industry.

8
Don't Forget to Give Back

In the intricate web of life and technology, the principle of *what goes around comes around*, or the *golden rule*, holds a profound significance. This principle, which is echoed in various forms throughout history and across cultures, teaches us to treat others as we would like to be treated. From the concept of Karma in Hinduism and Buddhism to the teachings of Confucianism, Christianity, and Islam, this universal tenet underscores the intertwined nature of our actions and their consequences.

In today's interconnected world, this principle takes on a new dimension as we explore it in the context of technical communities and societal contributions. As professionals in the **information technology (IT)** industry, we are uniquely positioned to make significant contributions to society. Our technical capabilities and financial resources can be leveraged to address a myriad of societal challenges.

The philosophy of *think globally, act locally* serves as a guiding principle in this endeavor. It encourages us to understand the global implications of our actions while focusing on making a difference within our local communities. This approach allows us to see the direct impact of our actions, fostering a sense of fulfillment and purpose.

This chapter aims to inspire and guide IT professionals in their journey of giving back. It provides insights into how they can use their skills and resources to contribute to technical communities and society at large. The discussion is rooted in the belief that every small action can ripple outwards, creating a wave of positive change that extends far beyond our immediate surroundings.

In this chapter, we will cover the following topics:

- The importance of giving back
- Giving back to technical communities
- Giving back to society
- The role of companies in giving back
- Overcoming challenges in giving back
- The future of giving back

> **Important note**
> Please note that this chapter focuses on a topic that can be deeply personal and I am sharing my personal views. You may entirely disagree or agree on a principle but have very different ways of putting it into practice. This is the beauty of the diverse population that shares our planet and I hope that you do not interpret this chapter as me saying that they are *wrong*.

The importance of giving back

Understanding the importance of giving back is the first step in our journey toward making a difference. When we give back, we are not just helping others, but also enriching our own lives. This aligns with the *golden rule*. It's a principle that fosters empathy, respect, and mutual growth.

In the context of technical communities, giving back can take many forms. It could be sharing knowledge through blog posts or webinars, contributing to open source projects, or mentoring aspiring professionals. These actions not only help others in their learning journey but also lead to our own personal and professional growth. They help us build new skills, broaden our perspectives, and foster a sense of belonging and community.

When it comes to society at large, giving back often involves leveraging our technical skills for social good. This could be developing an app that addresses a community issue, teaching coding skills to underprivileged students, or using data analysis to help a non-profit optimize its operations. These actions have the potential to create a significant societal impact.

Moreover, giving back also has a positive effect on our mental well-being. It gives us a sense of purpose and fulfillment, knowing that we are making a difference. It strengthens our connection with the community and helps us understand and appreciate diverse perspectives.

In essence, the importance of giving back lies in its mutual benefit – it's a two-way street. As we contribute to the betterment of technical communities and society, we also grow as individuals and professionals. We become part of something bigger than ourselves – a global movement toward creating a more inclusive and equitable world.

Now that we have established what is meant by giving back and why it is important, in the next section, we will look at giving back from the perspective of contributing back to technical communities.

Giving back to technical communities

In the realm of IT, the act of giving back takes on a unique significance. As professionals equipped with specialized skills and often substantial financial resources when compared with peers who chose different career paths, we have the potential to make impactful contributions to technical communities. These communities, which include forums, open source projects, and professional networks, thrive on collaboration and knowledge sharing. They serve as platforms for learning, innovation, and growth.

In this section, we will examine the following ways to give back to technical communities:

- Sharing knowledge
- Mentoring
- Contributing to open source projects
- Participating in forums and discussions

Let's get started!

Sharing knowledge

One of the most direct ways of giving back to these communities is through knowledge sharing. By sharing our knowledge, we not only help others in their learning journey but also reinforce our understanding of the subject matter. A senior CSA can contribute to sharing knowledge in several ways, as follows:

- *Educating* customers, partners, and colleagues on the benefits, challenges, and best practices of cloud computing, as well as the specific features and capabilities of different cloud platforms and services
- *Collaborating* with other CSAs and experts across different domains, industries, and regions to exchange ideas, insights, and feedback on cloud architectures and solutions
- *Publishing* articles, blogs, whitepapers, case studies, vlogs, and other resources that showcase the value, innovation, and impact of cloud solutions, as well as the lessons learned and recommendations from real-world projects and experiences
- *Presenting* at conferences, webinars, workshops, user groups, and other events that reach a wide and diverse audience of cloud enthusiasts, practitioners, and decision-makers, and inspire them to learn more and adopt cloud technologies

Mentoring

Mentoring is another powerful way of giving back. By guiding less experienced individuals in their career journey, we can help them navigate challenges, acquire new skills, and grow professionally. Mentoring can be a rewarding experience that allows us to make a direct impact on someone's career.

A senior CSA can mentor someone early in their career by sharing their insights and best practices, providing feedback and guidance, and helping them develop the skills and competencies needed for the role. Some of the ways a senior CSA can mentor a junior CSA are as follows:

- **Explaining the fundamentals of cloud computing**: A senior CSA can help a junior or aspiring CSA understand the basic concepts and principles of cloud computing, such as the different types of cloud services (SaaS, IaaS, and PaaS), the benefits and challenges of cloud adoption, and the common cloud architectures and design patterns.

- **Demonstrating how to use cloud tools and technologies**: A senior CSA can show a junior CSA how to use various cloud tools and technologies, such as AWS, Azure, Google Cloud, or other platforms, to create and manage cloud solutions. They can also teach them how to use cloud-specific tools, such as CloudFormation templates, cloud monitoring and security tools, and cloud development and testing tools.

- **Involving them in real-world projects**: A senior CSA can involve a junior CSA in real-world projects, where they can apply their knowledge and skills to solve real problems and deliver value to the clients. They can also assign them specific tasks and responsibilities, such as designing a cloud component, testing a cloud solution, or troubleshooting a cloud issue, and provide them with constructive feedback and suggestions.

- **Encouraging them to learn and grow**: A senior CSA can encourage a junior CSA to learn and grow by exposing them to new technologies and trends in cloud computing, recommending them relevant courses and resources, and supporting them in pursuing cloud certifications and accreditations. They can also help them set realistic and achievable goals, and celebrate their achievements and progress.

Contributing to open source projects

Open source projects are a cornerstone of technical communities. They provide valuable resources for learning and are often the driving force behind technological innovation. Contributing to these projects allows us to improve existing technologies, solve complex problems, and learn from other experienced professionals. Contributing to open source projects was discussed in *Chapter 5, Closing In on Opportunities*.

Participating in forums and discussions

Forums and discussions are platforms where individuals can ask questions, share ideas, and learn from each other. Participating in these platforms allows us to engage with a diverse group of professionals, broaden our perspectives, and stay updated on the latest trends and technologies. A senior CSA can contribute to forums and discussions by doing the following:

- *Sharing* their knowledge, experience, and insights on various cloud topics, challenges, and solutions with other cloud professionals and enthusiasts, and providing constructive feedback and guidance to those who seek help or advice.

- *Learning* from other cloud experts and peers, and staying updated on the latest trends, developments, and best practices in the cloud domain, as well as the specific cloud platforms and technologies they use or are interested in.

- *Engaging* in meaningful and respectful conversations that foster a sense of community, collaboration, and innovation among cloud practitioners, and that promote the adoption and advancement of cloud computing.

- *Participating* in various online and offline events, such as webinars, workshops, hackathons, meetups, and conferences, that offer opportunities to network, showcase, and discover cloud solutions, and to exchange ideas and opinions with other cloud enthusiasts and influencers.

In conclusion, giving back to technical communities is not just about making a difference in the lives of others – it's also about personal growth and satisfaction, as well as being part of a community that thrives on collaboration and mutual respect.

Having looked at contributions that you can make to technical communities, in the next section, we will explore ways that you can give back to society in general.

Giving back to society

IT professionals have a unique opportunity to use our skills and resources to make a significant impact on society. This impact can be realized in various ways, from leveraging our technical skills for social good to making financial contributions to causes that resonate with us. However, it's important to remember that giving back isn't limited to our professional skills.

In this section, we will discuss the following ways that you can give back to society:

- Leveraging personal skills and passions
- Teaching and mentoring
- Financial contributions
- Volunteering

Let's get started!

Leveraging personal skills and passions

Beyond our technical abilities, each of us has a unique set of personal skills and passions that can be used to benefit others. This could involve using our communication skills to advocate for important causes, leveraging our artistic talents to raise awareness about social issues, or using our organizational abilities to coordinate community events. These actions not only contribute to societal well-being but also provide us with an opportunity to express ourselves in meaningful ways.

Teaching and mentoring

Education is a powerful tool for societal change. As IT professionals, we can contribute to this change by teaching coding skills to underprivileged students, mentoring young people interested in technology, or even creating online courses that are accessible to all. However, teaching isn't limited to our professional expertise. Sharing knowledge about any subject we're passionate about can have a profound impact on others.

Financial contributions

While our technical skills are valuable, financial contributions also play a crucial role in societal change. This could involve donating to charities, sponsoring educational programs, or supporting research initiatives. Financial contributions, no matter how small, can make a big difference in the lives of those who need it most.

Volunteering

Volunteering our time and skills is another impactful way of giving back to society. This could involve participating in local community projects, offering pro bono IT services, or volunteering at events. But volunteering isn't just about offering our professional skills – it's about being present, lending a hand where it's needed, and making a difference in any way we can.

In conclusion, giving back to society is an integral part of being an IT professional – and being a human being. It's about using all our skills and resources – both professional and personal – to make a difference and create a better world for all. It's about thinking globally and acting locally – understanding the broader implications of our actions while making an impact within our communities.

In this section, we've focused heavily on things that you, as an individual, can do to give back. In the following section, we'll take a step back and look at what people can do collectively through association with a company that actively gives back.

The role of companies in giving back

Companies, particularly those in the IT industry, play a crucial role in cultivating a culture of giving back. They have the resources and influence to make significant contributions to both technical communities and society at large. This can be achieved through various initiatives, from **corporate social responsibility (CSR)** programs to employee volunteering and donation matching.

To set the stage for the kind of good that companies may choose to do, I would like to share the single moment that I took the greatest pride in being an employee of Microsoft. The date was March 4, 2020, and I was checking my email during a break for a customer design session in Singapore. In my inbox was an email announcing that the Redmond, WA campus would be temporarily closed due to the rapid spread of the COVID-19 virus and that all employees were to work from home as a temporary precaution. The part that made me proud, though, was that it went on to explain that vendors providing services such as janitorial, food, and maintenance would continue to be paid as if those services were being provided so that the vendors could, in turn, continue to pay their employees to limit the hardship caused by the shutdown. The reason that this struck me was that it's common for large companies to use contracted services specifically because it limits what a company is obligated to do for the people providing services. To me, this was a great example of a company choosing to do good.

In this section, we will review the following ways that companies may choose to participate in giving back:

- CSR
- Employee volunteering and donation matching
- Encouraging employee contributions to technical communities
- Partnerships with non-profit organizations

Let's get started!

CSR

CSR programs are one of the primary ways companies give back to society. These programs often involve initiatives aimed at improving societal well-being, such as sponsoring educational programs, supporting environmental sustainability projects, or investing in community development. By aligning their CSR initiatives with their business goals and values, companies can make a meaningful impact while also enhancing their brand reputation.

Employee volunteering and donation matching

Many companies encourage their employees to give back by offering volunteering opportunities and donation-matching programs. Volunteering allows employees to contribute their time and skills to causes they care about, fostering a sense of fulfillment and purpose. Donation matching programs, on the other hand, amplify the impact of employees' financial contributions by matching them with a corporate donation.

With both types of programs, the company gets the benefit of tuning, where it focuses on giving into areas where the company's employees are also actively giving, so there's the cultural benefit of employees knowing their employer is supporting the causes most relevant to them. As you learn about your company's giving programs, you are likely to find that they have a process to nominate non-profits that are meaningful to you for inclusion.

Encouraging employee contributions to technical communities

Companies can also support technical communities by encouraging their employees to share knowledge, mentor others, and contribute to open source projects. This not only benefits the community but also contributes to the professional growth of employees. Companies can facilitate this by providing resources, creating internal recognition programs, or allocating time for these activities.

Partnerships with non-profit organizations

Partnerships with non-profit organizations offer another avenue for companies to give back. Through these partnerships, companies can leverage their resources and expertise to support causes that align with their corporate values. This could involve developing tech solutions for non-profits, sponsoring events, or providing in-kind donations.

In conclusion, the role of companies in giving back is multifaceted and significant. By fostering a culture of giving back, companies not only contribute to societal progress but also enhance employee engagement, improve brand reputation, and strengthen community relations. It's about thinking globally as a corporate entity and enabling local action through employees and partnerships.

In this section, we explored ways that companies may choose to give back. Having looked at both individual and organizational ways to give back, in the next section, we will discuss challenges that sometimes hinder giving back.

Overcoming challenges in giving back

While the journey of giving back is rewarding, it's not without its challenges. These challenges can range from finding the time to volunteer to dealing with the complexities of open source contributions, to navigating the intricacies of societal issues. However, understanding these obstacles is the first step toward overcoming them and making a meaningful contribution.

Here are the specific areas where we will address challenges:

- Time management
- Navigating open source contributions
- Understanding societal issues
- Dealing with setbacks
- Balancing personal fulfillment and impact

Let's get started!

Time management

One of the most common challenges in giving back is finding the time. Between our professional responsibilities and personal commitments, it can be difficult to carve out time for volunteering or other forms of giving back. However, effective time management can help overcome this challenge. This could involve setting aside a specific time each week for volunteering or integrating giving-back activities into our daily routine.

Navigating open source contributions

Contributing to open source projects can be complex, particularly for those new to it. It involves understanding the project's code base, following contribution guidelines, and communicating effectively with other contributors. To overcome this challenge, it's helpful to start with smaller tasks, take the time to understand the project's dynamics, and seek help from the community when needed.

Understanding societal issues

When giving back to society, it's crucial to have a deep understanding of the issues we're trying to address. This requires research, empathy, and, often, direct engagement with affected communities. Overcoming this challenge involves continuous learning and listening to diverse perspectives.

Dealing with setbacks

In any form of giving back, there will be setbacks. Projects may not go as planned, or our efforts may not have the impact we hoped for. It's important to view these setbacks as learning opportunities rather than failures. Persistence and resilience are key to overcoming this challenge.

Balancing personal fulfillment and impact

Giving back should not only benefit society but also bring us personal fulfillment. Sometimes, finding activities that satisfy both can be challenging. To overcome this, we can explore different forms of giving back until we find those that align with our passions and values.

In this section, you've seen that while the path of giving back has its challenges, they are not insurmountable. With understanding, persistence, and a positive mindset, we can overcome these obstacles and make a significant impact in our technical communities and society at large. In the next section, we will consider potential future developments in giving back.

The future of giving back

As we look toward the future, the concept of giving back continues to evolve, particularly within the tech industry. The rapid advancement of technology, the increasing interconnectedness of our world, and the growing awareness of societal issues are all factors that are shaping the future of giving back.

As we consider the future of giving back, we will look at the following aspects:

- Leveraging emerging technologies
- Fostering a global community
- Addressing societal challenges
- Promoting inclusivity in tech

Let's get started!

Leveraging emerging technologies

Emerging technologies such as AI, blockchain, and virtual reality have the potential to revolutionize how we give back. They can be used to create innovative solutions for societal issues, enhance the effectiveness of charitable organizations, and even transform the way we volunteer. Let's take a quick look at how each may enhance or change giving back.

AI

AI is a collection of subfields related to the intelligence of machines as opposed to the intelligence of humans and strives to create systems that can reason, learn, plan, perceive, and communicate. Some of these subfields include ML, natural language processing, computer vision, robotics, and artificial neural networks. AI is in the midst of significant growth and there are already great examples of how various AI subfields will benefit from giving back:

- Orbis is a non-profit that brings people together to fight avoidable blindness. They have developed a tool powered by ML that can detect common eye diseases by examining digital images of the eye.

- The **United Nations Children's Fund** (**UNICEF**) is using natural language processing to generate text summaries of thousands of reports on children's well-being across the globe.

- The **World Wildlife Fund** (**WWF**) is using computer vision to detect and deter wildlife poachers in Africa and Asia using thermal cameras and drones.

Blockchain

Blockchain is a technology that allows data to be stored in a secure, transparent, and decentralized way. It is a type of distributed ledger that contains cryptographic mechanisms to validate blocks and avoid tampering. Some key ways that blockchain can help in giving back include using it to support efficient cash transfers, track donations, and create innovative results-based financing models where donations to charities are unlocked only when specific goals are met.

Virtual reality

Virtual reality is a technology that can create immersive and realistic simulations of various environments and scenarios. It can be used for various purposes, such as entertainment, education, training, therapy, and social change. Some potential use cases for virtual reality include providing immersive training for volunteers or beneficiaries of a cause, creating a sense of community between volunteers and beneficiaries who may be separated by long distances, and unique visual storytelling to help charities share stories about their work, impact, and vision.

As IT professionals, we have an exciting opportunity to be at the forefront of this transformation.

Fostering a global community

The increasing interconnectedness of our world is also shaping the future of giving back. It's enabling us to think globally and act locally on a scale like never before. Through online platforms and digital tools, we can collaborate with individuals and organizations across the globe, share knowledge with a worldwide audience, and have a global impact on our local communities.

Addressing societal challenges

As awareness of societal challenges grows, so does the importance of giving back. Issues such as climate change, inequality, and the digital divide require collective action and innovative solutions. In the future, giving back will not just be about contributing to our communities but also about addressing these global challenges.

Promoting inclusivity in tech

The tech industry has a crucial role to play in promoting inclusivity and diversity. By giving back through mentorship programs, educational initiatives, and open source contributions, we can help create a more inclusive tech community. This not only benefits underrepresented groups but also enriches the industry as a whole.

In conclusion, the future of giving back is promising and exciting. It's about leveraging technology for social good, fostering a global community of givers, addressing societal challenges, and promoting inclusivity in tech. As we navigate this future, let's take advantage of the opportunities we're given to make a difference.

Summary

As we conclude this exploration of giving back in the context of the IT industry, it's important to reflect on our key takeaways. The principle of *what goes around comes around*, or the *golden rule*, serves as our guiding philosophy. It reminds us that our actions toward others should reflect how we wish to be treated.

We've discussed the importance of giving back, both to technical communities and society at large. We've seen how our professional skills and personal passions can be leveraged to make a significant impact. We've also explored the role of companies in fostering a culture of giving back and the challenges that come with it.

Looking toward the future, we see a landscape full of potential. Emerging technologies offer new avenues for giving back, while the increasing interconnectedness of our world enables us to have a global impact on our local communities. As we navigate this future, we carry with us the philosophy of *think globally, act locally*.

In essence, giving back is more than just an act; it's a philosophy that can guide our professional and personal lives. It's about understanding our place in the world, recognizing the power of our actions, and taking responsibility for driving positive change. As we move forward, we should keep these principles in mind and continue on our journey of giving back.

Remember, every small action can ripple outwards, creating a wave of positive change that extends far beyond our immediate surroundings. So, let's start making those ripples.

Not only have you reached the end of this chapter, but you've also reached the end of this book! Throughout this book, we've examined the CSA role, education and experiences that contribute to becoming a CSA, technical and non-technical skills needed to be a successful CSA, starting and building your CSA career, and discussed giving back. Please accept our heartfelt well wishes in your journey to becoming a CSA and, of course, don't forget to refresh your skillsets periodically.

Index

www.packtpub.com

Subscribe to our online digital library for full access to over 7,000 books and videos, as well as industry leading tools to help you plan your personal development and advance your career. For more information, please visit our website.

Why subscribe?

- Spend less time learning and more time coding with practical eBooks and Videos from over 4,000 industry professionals

- Improve your learning with Skill Plans built especially for you

- Get a free eBook or video every month

- Fully searchable for easy access to vital information

- Copy and paste, print, and bookmark content

Did you know that Packt offers eBook versions of every book published, with PDF and ePub files available? You can upgrade to the eBook version at packtpub.com and as a print book customer, you are entitled to a discount on the eBook copy. Get in touch with us at customercare@packtpub.com

 for more details.

At www.packtpub.com, you can also read a collection of free technical articles, sign up for a range of free newsletters, and receive exclusive discounts and offers on Packt books and eBooks.

Other Books You May Enjoy

If you enjoyed this book, you may be interested in these other books by Packt:

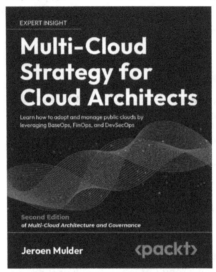

Multi-Cloud Strategy for Cloud Architects

Jeroen Mulder

ISBN: 978-1-80461-673-4

- Choose the right cloud platform with the help of use cases.
- Master multi-cloud concepts, including IaC, SaaS, PaaS, and CaC.
- Use the techniques and tools offered by Azure, AWS, and GCP to integrate security.
- Maximize cloud potential with Azure, AWS, and GCP frameworks for enterprise architecture.
- Use FinOps to define cost models and optimize cloud costs with showback and chargeback.

Microsoft Power Platform Solution Architect's Handbook

Hugo Herrera

ISBN: 978-1-80181-933-6

- Cement the foundations of your applications using best practices.
- Use proven design, build, and go-live strategies to ensure success.
- Lead requirements gathering and analysis with confidence.
- Secure even the most complex solutions and integrations
- Ensure compliance between the Microsoft ecosystem and your business.
- Build resilient test and deployment strategies to optimize solutions.

Packt is searching for authors like you

If you're interested in becoming an author for Packt, please visit `authors.packtpub.com` and apply today. We have worked with thousands of developers and tech professionals, just like you, to help them share their insight with the global tech community. You can make a general application, apply for a specific hot topic that we are recruiting an author for, or submit your own idea.

Share your thoughts

Now you've finished *Cloud Solution Architect's Career Master Plan*, we'd love to hear your thoughts! Scan the QR code below to go straight to the Amazon review page for this book and share your feedback or leave a review on the site that you purchased it from.

`https://packt.link/r/1-805-12971-6`

Your review is important to us and the tech community and will help us make sure we're delivering excellent quality content.

Download a free PDF copy of this book

Thanks for purchasing this book!

Do you like to read on the go but are unable to carry your print books everywhere?

Is your eBook purchase not compatible with the device of your choice?

Don't worry, now with every Packt book you get a DRM-free PDF version of that book at no cost.

Read anywhere, any place, on any device. Search, copy, and paste code from your favorite technical books directly into your application.

The perks don't stop there, you can get exclusive access to discounts, newsletters, and great free content in your inbox daily

Follow these simple steps to get the benefits:

1. Scan the QR code or visit the link below

https://packt.link/free-ebook/9781805129714

2. Submit your proof of purchase
3. That's it! We'll send your free PDF and other benefits to your email directly

www.ingramcontent.com/pod-product-compliance
Lightning Source LLC
Chambersburg PA
CBHW080536060326
40690CB00022B/5142

* 9 7 8 1 8 0 5 1 2 9 7 1 4 *